国际胜任力英语系列

国际胜任力英语教程

——国际理解

总主编　王　昊

主　编　王浦程

副主编　高亚娟　李玲玲

U0331253

清華大学出版社

北京

内 容 简 介

本书采用模块化设计，以全球治理议题为主线，通过案例分析、讨论等形式，帮助学生深入理解全球治理的复杂性和多样性。本书包含知识、技能、态度和价值观四个主要维度，共八个单元，围绕全球治理的核心议题展开，如教育、创新、和平等，通过"理解全球议题"等板块，引导学生深入探讨和分析全球性问题。本书每个单元配套音频资源以及单元小测，读者可先扫描封底的"文泉云盘防盗码"解锁资源后，再扫描书中对应处的二维码获取听力资源，同时可通过"文泉考试"进行单元测验。

本书使用对象主要是高等院校的本科学生，也适合其他英语爱好者自学使用。

版权所有，侵权必究。举报：010-62782989，beiqinquan@tup.tsinghua.edu.cn。

图书在版编目（CIP）数据

国际胜任力英语教程.国际理解 / 王昊总主编；王浦程主编；高亚娟，李玲玲副主编 . -- 北京：清华大学出版社，2024.7. --（国际胜任力英语系列）.
ISBN 978-7-302-66767-4

Ⅰ. H319.39

中国国家版本馆 CIP 数据核字第 2024ZR7657 号

责任编辑：徐博文
封面设计：李伯骥
责任校对：王荣静
责任印制：刘 菲

出版发行：清华大学出版社
      网　　　址：https://www.tup.com.cn, https://www.wqxuetang.com
      地　　　址：北京清华大学学研大厦 A 座　　　　邮　编：100084
      社 总 机：010-83470000　　　　　　　　　　邮　购：010-62786544
      投稿与读者服务：010-62776969，c-service@tup.tsinghua.edu.cn
      质量反馈：010-62772015，zhiliang@tup.tsinghua.edu.cn
印 装 者：三河市龙大印装有限公司
经　　销：全国新华书店
开　　本：185mm×260mm　　　　印　张：7.75　　　　字　数：176 千字
版　　次：2024 年 7 月第 1 版　　　　　　　　印　次：2024 年 7 月第 1 次印刷
定　　价：59.00 元

产品编号：103912-01

前言

  "国际胜任力英语系列"以《大学英语教学指南（2020 版）》为指导，对接《中国英语能力等级量表》，落实立德树人根本任务，以中国特色的全球治理理念和实践为蓝本，探讨人类命运共同体等本土理念对全球性问题的贡献，旨在培养熟悉党和国家方针政策、了解我国国情、具有全球视野、熟练运用外语、通晓国际规则、精通国际谈判的国际化应用型人才。本系列教程通过讲好中国故事、融合学科交叉和探索实践新技术三方面，积极应对党和国家对新时代、新技术和新发展背景下的人才培养需求，即"为谁培养人""培养什么样的人"和"怎样培养人"的问题。本系列教程在内容上一方面体现全球治理的重要议题，帮助学生了解当今国际社会所面临的共同问题，拓宽学生的全球视野，培养跨文化交际能力；另一方面，结合学生实际需求，选择难度适中的语言材料和相关话题，各单元之间体现了递进性和连贯性，使学生能够循序渐进地掌握英语技能和知识。本系列教程以任务为导向设计真实情境下的交际任务，激发学生的学习兴趣。练习任务包括听力、口语对话、阅读理解、写作等，帮助学生将语言运用到实际情境中。

  本系列教程积极回应新文科建设，以中国价值为核心，主动将中国智慧有机融入全球治理视角下的国际议题，通过学科交叉进行新知识生产体系的构建，在加深学生领悟本土价值的同时也提升了全球胜任力。本系列教程涵盖多个全球治理相关学科和领域的内容，使学生全面了解全球治理的多维度和复杂性，有效提升学生的跨学科知识素养。新文科建设回应科技文明的进步，将传统文科与技术的互动作为其核心之一。本系列教程在任务设计、素材选取、语言处理等多方面推进人文与技术的互动融通。具体而言，本系列教程以数字技术和人工智能为方法和手段，为学生构建大学英语教育新形态，将全球治理相关内容与英语语言知识和技能有机结合，在教授语言的同时还通过相关学科内容的介绍和讨论，拓展学生的学科知识面，形成一定的学科意识，提升学科语言能力。通过内容语言在顶层设计和教学实践中的创新性融合，本系列教程旨在培养学生的全球治理学科知识、语言能力。同时，从全人教育的视角，提升学生的世界观、人生观和价值观等个人素养。

教程特色

本系列教程引导学生拓展全球视野、理解多元文化交流场景中的语言使用习惯和跨文化交际技巧，通过引入大量的实践案例，如国际组织的运作机制和全球共性问题的应对措施等，一方面使学生了解不同国家和地区在全球治理中的角色和影响，另一方面帮助学生在国际交流中更加自信、更加有效地表达自己。本系列教程依托多媒体技术，采用以学为中心的设计思路，引入任务式、项目式和跨文化交际等多元学习形态，鼓励学生开展课内外、校内外和国内外的多维度合作学习，打造全方位、多元化的大学英语教育体验。

本系列教程共三册，分别为《国际胜任力英语教程：国际理解》《国际胜任力英语教程：国际传播》《国际胜任力英语教程：国际交流》。本系列教程的编排借鉴内容语言融合教育理念，主张语言知识技能和跨学科知识素养的综合培养。在主题设计方面，《国际胜任力英语教程：国际理解》涵盖八个主题：脱贫、教育、创新、和平、公正、道德、健康、全球公民;《国际胜任力英语教程：国际传播》涵盖八个主题：全球气候、资源可持续、水资源、物种多样性、森林砍伐、自然灾害、废物回收、绿色发展;《国际胜任力英语教程：国际交流》涵盖八个主题：政府间国际组织、非政府间国际组织、演讲技巧与礼仪、国际交流与合作、国际学术研讨、国际学术会议、国际学术合作、学术伦理与诚信。每个单元设定明确的教学目标，包括语言技能（听、说、读、写、译）、语言知识（词汇、语言功能）、交际能力（听力理解、口语表达、阅读理解、写作表达）、课程思政等。

编写团队

　　本系列教程由浙江外国语学院应用外语学院的核心教师团队组成编写组，学院教学副院长担任编写组组组长，院长助理和系主任担任主要编写人员，明确每一层级权责分工，定期举行主要编写成员间的编写交流会议。同时，编写组邀请校外长期从事大学英语教材编写的专家担任学术顾问。本系列教程从主题内容的初步构想、编写大纲的制定，再到书稿的细致审校，均得到了清华大学出版社领导及编辑团队的大力支持。在此，我们对他们表示衷心感谢。

　　鉴于编者能力所限，教程中可能仍存在疏漏与不足之处，我们诚挚地邀请广大师生不吝赐教，为本系列教程的完善提出宝贵意见和建议。

编写组

2024.3

CONTENTS 目录

Unit 8　Global Citizenship ·········· 101

Unit 1

Poverty Alleviation

PART **I** Listening and Speaking

Section 1 Pre-Listening Activity

Directions: *Browse the questions below and discuss one of the following questions with your partner. List the key information, and share your opinion with the class.*

(1) Have you heard stories of hunger or poverty from the older generation? Tell these stories.

(2) Do people in cities also face poverty, and what special problems do they have?

(3) In your understanding, what are some effective methods for reducing poverty?

(4) Which government policies have proven most effective in reducing poverty?

(5) What roles does education play in alleviating poverty?

(6) How can technology and innovation be harnessed to address poverty, especially in terms of providing education, healthcare, and economic opportunities?

Section 2 Listening Comprehension

Passage One

1. Directions: *Listen to the following passage. Fill in the blanks with what you hear.*

In the mountains of Northern Laos, life keeps getting better and better for the (1) _____ of Ban Xor. According to Khamchan Boudvinai, deputy village chief, everyone has a little more money to spend these days. In 2017, the Ban Xor village was chosen to pilot a (2) _____ poverty alleviation project. Two hours' drive north of capital Vientiane, it was one of the first (3) _____ in Laos to benefit from China's years of hard work to (4) _____ poverty at home.

Khamchan has seen for himself how rural communities in China were (5) _____. Khamchan returned from his visits, not just interested in modern agriculture, but determined to transform his village. He was convinced that the Chinese experience in poverty eradication would be (6) _____ in Laos. And that there was more to it than just growing more crops. "I saw (7) _____ growing in well-managed terraces that had become tourist attractions. It was thought-provoking."

Of the some 2,000 people who live in Ban Xor, half still make less than 700 US dollars a year. However, in the past three years, (8) _____ and infrastructure have improved. A new bridge has been built.

The village has better public (9) _____. And village affairs are much better managed. In fact, the villagers organize, supervise and manage themselves as a cooperative. The rice crop in the village was never enough, but since people (10) _____ to corn and cassava, the harvest improved, so did their incomes along with it, according to villager Ka Sidavongxay.

2. Directions: *Listen to the passage again. Decide whether the statements are true (T) or false (F).*

(1) Khamchan went to China twice and got some training in commercial management.

( )

(2) Khamchan returned from his visits to China and got interested in modern agriculture. ( )

(3) Villagers started to plant corn and cassava, which improved the harvest and their incomes. ( )

(4) The teams in this village are learning from China about how to raise cattle, grow corn and cassava, and weave cloth. ( )

(5) Khamchan was impressed by the good relationship between Chinese officials and villagers. ( )

Passage Two

Directions: *Listen to the following passage. Fill in the blanks with the words that you hear.*

What Is Poverty?

Poverty involves more than the lack of income and (1) _____ resources to ensure sustainable livelihoods. Its manifestations include (2) _____ and malnutrition, limited access to (3) _____ and other basic services, (4) _____ discrimination and exclusion, as well as the lack of participation in (5) _____. In 2015, more than (6) _____ million people lived below the international poverty line. Around 10 percent of the world population (pre-pandemic) was living in (7) _____ poverty and struggling to fulfil the most basic needs like health, education, and access to (8) _____ and sanitation (公共卫生), to name a few.

There were (9) _____ women aged 25 to 34 living in poverty for every 100 men of the same age group, and more than 160 million (10) _____ will be at risk of continuing to live in extreme poverty by 2030.

Poverty Facts and Figures

According to the most recent (1) _____ in 2015, 10 percent of the world's population or 734 million people lived on less than (2) $_____ a day.

(3) _____ Asia and sub-Saharan Africa are expected to see the largest increases in extreme poverty, with additional 32 million and 26 million people, respectively, living (4) _____ the international poverty line as a result of the pandemic.

The (5) _____ of the world's workers living in extreme poverty fell by half over the last decade from 14.3 percent in 2010 to 7.1% in 2019.

Even before COVID-19, baseline projections suggested that 6 percent of the (6) _____ population would still be living in extreme poverty in 2030, missing the (7) _____ of ending poverty. The fallout from the pandemic threatens to push over 70 million people into extreme poverty.

One out of five children lives in extreme poverty, and the (8) _____ effects of poverty and deprivation in the early years have consequences that can last a (9) _____.

In 2016, 55 percent of the world's population—about 4 billion people—did not benefit from any form of social (10) _____.

Strategies for Better Listening

Listening Skill: Getting Meaning from Context—Words, Synonyms and Paraphrases, Transitions

When you listen to people talking in English, it is probably difficult to understand all the words. However, you can usually get a general idea of what they are saying. How? By using *clues* that help you *guess*. These include:

Words,
Synonyms and paraphrases,
Transitions.

Many tests such as the TOEFL® iBT measure your academic listening and speaking abilities. This activity will develop your social and academic conversation skills, and provide a foundation for the success in a variety of standardized tests.

Exercises

1. Directions: *Discuss with your partner to find out how you have solved each blank in Passage One of Listening Comprehension. Then listen to the recording again and put down sentences illustrating the strategies. The teacher may wantyou to share the clues that help you get to the right words. The first has been done for you as an example.*

Example:

(1) Words

Khamchan returned from his visits, not just interested in modern agriculture, but determined to transform his village. He was convinced that the Chinese experience in poverty eradication would be _____ in Laos. And that there was more to it than just growing more crops.

Clues: The key words *transform* and *Chinese experience* provide the logic reference to help fill Blank Number 6 in Passage One.

(2) Synonyms and paraphrases

_____

_____

_____

(3) Transitions

_____

_____

_____

2. Directions: *Listen to the following four conversations. When you hear the question, please stop the recording and choose the best answer. In the clues column, write the words that can help you choose the answer. Then listen to the last part of each conversation to check the correct answer.*

Answers	Clues
(1) A. Going to the post office. B. Their grades in a course. C. Parents coming to visit. D. Going to the beach.	

(Continued)

Answers	Clues
(2) A. He doesn't like his major. B. He isn't going to graduate on time. C. His parents are disappointed. D. He's only in his third year.	
(3) A. A physician. B. A professor. C. A student advisor. D. A teaching assistant.	
(4) A. The student wrote an excellent essay. B. The student plagiarized a large part of her essay. C. The student is a very original writer. D. The student used too many words.	

PART **II** Reading

Section 1　Pre-reading Activity

1. Directions: *The passage you are going to read talks about "reducing rural poverty". In groups, make a list of common causes of poverty and share it with the class.*

Causes of poverty...

2. Directions: *The following are a few lines from the passage. In your opinion, what are they talking about?*

(1) "They also provided good rice seeds and fertilizer and taught me planting techniques..."

(2) "Every mouth has food and every pocket, money."

(3) "Our hybrid rice yields are twice as much as the local varieties."

(4) "We are very grateful for the work of the Chinese expert teams."

China Boosts Africa's Fight Against Poverty^①

On a **sultry** afternoon, Charles Mana, a farmer in Burundi's northwestern Bubanza Province, was busy adding a handful of grass to the cattle **trough** in the backyard of his newly built rural home, a spacious single-floor **bungalow** with freshly painted **lime** walls.

About a dozen hens were running around. Pointing to them, he said that the chickens had been given to his family by Chinese **agricultural** experts. "They also provided good rice seeds and fertilizer and taught me planting techniques so that I have enough food to feed my children," the 43-year-old father of six added.

Four years ago, Mana began growing **hybrid** rice introduced from China under the guidance of Chinese agricultural experts. Since then, his farmland has also increased from half a hectare to five hectares in Ninga, a village in the **Commune** of Gihanga. "Next, I want to buy more land, more cows, as well as several new water pumps when the dry season comes," said Mana, **asserting** that this was "unthinkable" in the days when food was even **scarce**, before the arrival of Chinese expert teams.

Known as the "heart of Africa", the country of Burundi has a **tropical** climate with abundant rainfall. Its natural conditions are favorable to rice production, but the low **yield** of local rice production causes food shortages. To address the challenge, China has been **implementing** technical **cooperation** programs in Burundi since August 2009, sending a total of 45 experts to the African country in five **batches** to help develop agriculture.

The Chinese experts are currently planting hybrid rice in 22 villages in the country in an effort to help realize Burundian President Evariste Ndayishimiye's slogan—"Every mouth has food and every pocket, money".

The experts have visited fields in all 14 rice-growing provinces of the country to conduct research and **trial**s, and successfully selected and introduced eight varieties of rice seeds adapted to the local conditions. In this way, they have helped effectively

---

① From *China Daily*.

address the problem of yield reduction or even extinction caused by rice **plague** in the mountainous areas of Burundi.

The Chinese experts also helped establish the first demonstration village of rice **cultivation** for **poverty alleviation** in Ninga village, where hybrid rice was grown for five **consecutive** seasons. Since hybrid rice was planted there, the village has increased its rice production by 1,661 **metric** tons, resulting in improved income for local households.

"Our hybrid rice yields are twice as much as the local varieties," Chinese expert Jiang Daiming said. "Rice yields here used to be only two to three tons per hectare, while the introduced disease-**resistant** variants can yield four to five tons per hectare, sometimes even seven tons."

To help Burundi build an independent and **sustainable** rice industry, Chinese experts have also conducted 82 training sessions in the country, training 3,050 people. Among them are dozens of bright young Burundians who are using the skills they have learned to help lift villagers out of poverty throughout the country.

Ernest Irankunda, a young man from Ninga, gave up the opportunity to attend university out of a sense of duty to his family and decided to learn rice cultivation techniques from Chinese experts. Now he has become a local expert in rice cultivation and was recently hired by the government to lead a team to share farming experience in the neighboring Democratic Republic of the Congo.

Agricultural cooperation with a view to reducing rural poverty in Africa has been an important area of China-Africa cooperation in recent years. During the 8th **Ministerial** Conference of the Forum on China-Africa Cooperation held a year ago in Senegal, China announced that it will implement the poverty reduction and agricultural development program with Africa over the next three years.

As part of the program, China will send 500 agricultural experts to Africa, set up a number of joint centers for modern **agrotechnology** exchange, demonstration and training in China, and encourage Chinese institutions and companies to build demonstration villages in Africa that support agricultural development and poverty reduction.

In October, such a village was **inaugurated** in the Matangi Tisa village in Kenya's Nakuru County. The chief official for agriculture in the county, Fredrick Owino, while welcoming the **initiative**, said that the project will promote China's advanced farming technologies in Kenya, **boosting** agricultural production and reducing poverty.

Also, last month, a Demonstration Village for China-Africa Agricultural Development and Poverty Reduction was set up at the Shimwengwe village in Zambia's Lusaka province. Through the project, villagers will be equipped with the knowledge and small-scale technologies to improve their productivity, especially in **rearing** chickens.

"We are very grateful for the work of the Chinese expert teams," said Prosper Dodiko, permanent secretary of Burundi's Ministry of Environment, Agriculture and Livestock, adding that besides hybrid rice, Chinese experts have also introduced apple trees and promoted **poultry** farming, **aquaculture**, and rice-fish farming. "Next year, Burundi's agricultural development is ready to enter another stage, where we will develop irrigation systems and agricultural mechanization. I am glad that Chinese experts are here to help us."

(832 words)

 New Words

sultry	/ˈsʌltrɪ/	adj.	闷热潮湿的
trough	/trɒf/	n.	饮水槽；饲料槽
bungalow	/ˈbʌŋɡəˌləʊ/	n.	平房
lime	/laɪm/	n.	石灰；酸橙
hybrid	/ˈhaɪbrɪd/	n.	杂交种；混合物
		adj.	杂交的；混合的
commune	/kəˈmjuːn/	n.	社群；群体
assert	/əˈsɜːt/	v.	坚称，断言
scarce	/skeəs/	adj.	缺乏的，不足的
tropical	/ˈtrɒpɪk(ə)l/	adj.	热带的
yield	/jiːld/	n.	产量
		v.	出产；屈服
implement	/ˈɪmplɪment/	v.	实施；执行
cooperation	/kəʊˌɒpəˈreɪʃ(ə)n/	n.	合作，协作
batch	/bætʃ/	n.	一批
trial	/ˈtraɪəl/	n.	试验；审判
plague	/pleɪɡ/	n.	瘟疫；祸患
cultivation	/ˌkʌltɪˈveɪʃ(ə)n/	n.	耕作；种植
poverty	/ˈpɒvəti/	n.	贫穷
alleviation	/əˌliːviˈeɪʃn/	n.	减轻，缓和
consecutive	/kənˈsekjətɪv/	adj.	连续的
metric	/ˈmetrɪk/	adj.	公制的
resistant	/rɪˈzɪstənt/	adj.	抵制的

sustainable	/sə'steɪnəb(ə)l/	*adj.*	可持续的
ministerial	/ˌmɪnɪ'stɪəriəl/	*adj.*	部长的
agrotechnology	/ˌægrəʊtek'nɒlədʒɪ/	*n.*	农业技术
inaugurate	/ɪ'nɔːgjəreɪt/	*v.*	为……举行落成典礼；开创
initiative	/ɪ'nɪʃətɪv/	*n.*	倡议；主动权
boost	/buːst/	*v.*	促进；推动
rear	/rɪə(r)/	*v.*	饲养，养育
poultry	/'pəʊltri/	*n.*	家禽
aquaculture	/'ækwəkʌltʃə(r)/	*n.*	水产养殖

 Phrases and Expressions

under the guidance of	在……的指引下
be favorable to	有利于
in an effort to	为了；努力
result in	导致，结果是
lift sb. out of poverty	使……摆脱贫困
out of a sense of duty	出于责任感
set up	设置；成立；开办
be equipped with	装备有

Section 2　Reading Comprehension

1. Directions: *Read the passage as quickly as you can. Answer the questions.*

(1) Who is Charles Mana?

(2) Who is Jiang Daiming?

(3) Which places in the world are mentioned?

(4) Which causes of poverty from your list in Pre-reading Activity 1 are mentioned?

(5) Which of your ideas about the lines in Pre-reading Activity 2 is correct? Which is not?

2. Directions: *Read the passage again. Decide whether the following statements are true (T) or false (F). Correct the false ones.*

(1) Charles Mana's farmland has increased ten times since he began growing hybrid rice introduced from China.　　　　　　　　　　　　　　　　　　　　　　　　(　　)

(2) Burundi has a shortage of food due to unfavorable natural conditions for rice production. ( )

(3) China has been implementing technical cooperation programs in Burundi since August 2009 to help develop agriculture. ( )

(4) Chinese experts are planting hybrid rice in 14 villages in Burundi. ( )

(5) Chinese experts have successfully selected and introduced eight varieties of rice seeds adapted to the local conditions in Burundi. ( )

(6) The village of Ninga increased its rice production by 1,661 metric tons after five consecutive seasons of planting hybrid rice. ( )

(7) China will be sending 500 agricultural experts to Africa as part of a poverty reduction and agricultural development program. ( )

(8) The Demonstration Village in Zambia will focus on improving rice cultivation techniques. ( )

What Do You Think?

3. Directions: Discuss the followings in small groups or pairs. Then report to the class.

(1) What factors enable the success of the Chinese experts' efforts to improve rice production in Burundi, and how might these factors be replicated in other development projects?

(2) What other technical cooperation programs are being implemented in developing countries to help solve food and agriculture-related issues?

(3) How effective are demonstration villages and modern agrotechnology centers in promoting sustainable agriculture, and what challenges might arise in implementing these initiatives in various regions of Africa?

(4) What role do local officials and community leaders play in ensuring the success of China-Africa agricultural cooperation, and how can they collaborate with Chinese experts to develop locally appropriate solutions for poverty reduction and agricultural development?

(5) What are some of the potential drawbacks or criticisms of relying on technical expertise from foreign countries to solve local food production challenges?

(6) In what ways might China-Africa agricultural cooperation contribute to broader

efforts to achieve the United Nations Sustainable Development Goals, particularly those related to poverty eradication, food security, and sustainable agriculture?

Vocabulary

4. Directions: *Read the following sentences. Search the passage for words that mean the same as those underlined.*

(1) The car uses **a mixture of** electricity and gasoline to power its engine.

(2) The scientist is exploring ways to enhance the **crop output** of the experimental plant.

(3) The charity's goal is to provide aid and support to **ease off** the suffering of people in war-torn regions.

(4) Taking a break and getting some fresh air can help **improve** your productivity.

(5) The Prime Minister held a **cabinet** meeting to discuss the latest economic developments.

5. Directions: *Complete the following sentences with the correct forms of words from the passage.*

(1) The business leader had to **a** _____ his position on the proposed merger with a strong and confident tone to let everyone know where he stood on the matter.

(2) The project was completed successfully thanks to all team members **c** _____ with each other, communicating effectively and working together towards a common goal.

(3) It's essential to take necessary steps to **s** _____ the environment's fragile ecosystem by reducing carbon emissions and protecting natural resources for future generations.

(4) The Belt and Road **I** _____ aims to enhance regional connectivity and promote economic cooperation through infrastructure development, trade, and investment, fostering greater cultural exchange and mutual learning among participating countries.

(5) Gardeners **c** _____ plants meticulously, giving attention to soil conditions, light exposure, and temperature to achieve optimal growth and yield, resulting in beautiful and bountiful gardens.

(6) It can be challenging to **r** _____ the temptation of instant gratification, but

the ability to delay gratification is vital for achieving long-term goals and building self-discipline.

(7) The athlete won three **c** _____ gold medals in the Olympic games, showcasing not only his skill and determination but also his ability to sustain excellence under immense pressure and competition.

(8) The residents of the small **c** _____ had a strong sense of community, with everyone helping each other through the ups and downs of life, creating a close-knit and supportive environment.

6. Directions: *Complete the following sentences by selecting suitable phrases in the box.*

lift people out of poverty	be favorable to	under the guidance of
in an effort to	result in	out of a sense of duty
set up	be equipped with	

(1) Modern classrooms should _____ the latest technology, such as interactive whiteboards and tablets, to engage students and provide them with a dynamic and interactive learning experience.

(2) Not getting adequate sleep can _____ decreased productivity, irritability, and an increased risk of accidents or health problems in the long run.

(3) Efforts to improve education and provide job training programs can _____, empowering them to build better lives for themselves and their families.

(4) The warm and sunny weather _____ outdoor activities like hiking and picnicking, encouraging people to spend more time outside and enjoy nature.

(5) _____ promote eco-friendly practices, many individuals are adopting sustainable habits such as using reusable bags and bottles, reducing food waste, and conserving energy.

PART **III** Understanding Global Issues

Strategies for Better Speaking

Speaking Skill: Interpreting a Photograph

Photographs are easy to make with smartphones nowadays, and a good photo can always provide important information with even a simple glance. When interpreting the message in a photo, attention should be given to location (in which country or place), the number/features/actions of people, the center/focus of the picture, the peripheral objects, and a brief summary. The following sentence patterns are for your reference.

1) **Location** : I think this picture was taken/shot in...

2) **People (number/features/actions):** There are... people in this picture.

3) **Message in the centre:** In the middle of the picture/the first thing comes to my eyes is somebody doing something (be specific). He is wearing...(be specific).

4) **Message of peripheral objects:** At the bottom of the picture; on the left/right side of the picture; in the foreground/background of the picture.

5) **Summary:** It seems like.../In my view...

6) **Prediction:** What is probably going to happen? That would come in at one point. I think they're probably to... next/in future.

Photograph Sample

Sample Story Structures

Paragraph 1   This photo was probably taken in... as...

Paragraph 2   It speaks of the poverty issue in/of...

Paragraph 3   To eradicate..., I think... maybe...

Exercise

Directions: *Work with your partner and come up with a 3-minute story that features the topic of poverty, following the seven steps below. Please also refer to the four questions below as your prompts.*

Step 1: Brainstorm with your partner to narrow the topic down to a specific case.

Step 2: Search the Internet for a photo that best illustrates the issue.

Step 3: Interpret the photo with strategies learned above/in the Speaking Skill Section.

Step 4: Weave the interpretation into the story, and use as many words as you can from the Reading section.

Step 5: Tell your partner the story, and switch roles when you finish.

Step 6: Polish the better/more interesting story between you two.

Step 7: Be prepared to share your story in front of the whole class.

(1) Can you provide the background information of these places, including their names, population, annual income, etc.?

(2) What are the poverty issues in those rural areas in China?

(3) In what ways have these poverty issues impacted on those rural areas?

(4) What are some of the ways you can use to help with those issues?

Unit 2

Education

PART **I** Listening and Speaking

Section 1 Pre-listening Activity

Directions: *Browse the questions below and discuss one of the following questions with your partner. List the key information, and share your opinion with the class.*

(1) Is artificial intelligence technology (e.g. ChatGPT) killing or underscoring the importance of traditional education?

(2) How can students overcome financial and geographical barriers to access quality education?

(3) How can governments ensure equitable distribution of educational resources across urban and rural areas?

(4) How can the concept of lifelong learning be better integrated into society to encourage continuous education beyond formal schooling?

(5) How can educators address the diverse needs of students, including those from different cultural backgrounds, learning abilities, and socio-economic statuses?

(6) What roles should mental health education play in formal education systems?

Section 2 Listening Comprehension

Passage One

Directions: *Listen to the following passage. Fill in the blanks with what you hear.*

The Communist Party of China Central Committee and the State Council recently issued a (1) _____ for the country's education development in the coming decade. China's Education Modernization 2035 plan sets the direction for the development of the education sector so that its overall (2) _____ and international influence are strengthened. It sets the objectives of establishing a modern education system of (3) _____ learning, with universal quality (4) _____ education, balanced (5) _____ education, as well as enhanced (6) _____ education and more competitive higher education. Education for those with (7) _____ should also be improved, so that the education system better serves the whole society.

On that basis, the education sector will further improve for (8) _____ years, with the aim of realizing its overall modernization by 2035, so as to make China a power in terms of human (9) _____ and talents, which will in turn provide a solid foundation for realizing the country's goal of being a fully developed nation by (10) _____.

Passage Two

1. Directions: *Listen to a passage about UNESCO. Answer the following questions in your own words.*

(1) What's the full name of UNESCO?

(2) What's the main purpose of UNESCO?

2. Direction: *Listen to the passage again. Decide whether the statements are true (T) or false (F).*

(1) The Sustainable Development Goals are part of UNESCO's 2030 Agenda.　　　 (　)

(2) Nazi Germany and its allies met in the United Kingdom for the Conference of Allied Ministers of Education (CAME).　　　 (　)

(3) Because World War II was approaching to the end, some European countries started to look for ways and means to rebuild their education systems.　　　 (　)

(4) Representatives from 44 countries decided to create an organization that would embody a genuine culture of peace in November 1945.　　　 (　)

(5) In the eyes of the representatives, establishing the "intellectual and moral solidarity of mankind" could prevent the outbreak of another world war.　　　 (　)

Strategies for Better Listening

Listening Skill: Getting Meaning from Context—Stressed Words, Intonation, the Knowledge of the Culture, Speaker and Situation

When listening to lectures or monologues, words, synonyms, and paraphrases can easily help decide the main information conveyed. However, the stressed words, intonation, the knowledge of the culture, speaker and situation, as well as the speaker's tone of voice, such as the speaker's attitude and emotion can help understand the hidden information.

Exercises

1. Directions: *Discuss with your partner to find out how you have solved each blank in Passage One of Listening Comprehension. Then listen again and put down sentences illustrating the strategies. The teacher may invite you to share the clues that help you get to the right words. The first one has been done for you as an example.*

Example:

(1) Clue(s): Words & your knowledge of the culture and situation

China's Education Modernization 2035 plan sets the direction for the development of the education sector so that its overall (2) _____ and international influence are strengthened. It sets the objectives of establishing a modern education system of (3) _____ learning, with universal quality (4) _____ education, balanced (5) _____ education, as well as enhanced (6) _____ education and more competitive higher education.

Analysis: The **stressed words** *objectives* and *education system* provide the logic reference to help fill the blanks. The phrases following the education system are parallel in form, thus may also be parallel and systematic in content. Based on the pronunciation and the knowledge about education, it's not that challenging then to decide the words missing are lifelong learning, pre-schooling, compulsory, and vocational.

(2) Stressed words

_____

_____

_____

(3) Intonation

_____

_____

_____

(4) The knowledge of the culture, speaker, or situation

_____

_____

_____

2. Directions: *Listen to the following three conversations. When you hear the question, please stop the recording and choose the best answer. In the clues column, write the words that can help you choose the answer. Then listen to the last part of each conversation to check the correct answer.*

Answers	Clues
(1) A. A neighbor. B. The apartment manager. C. Donna's father. D. A repairman.	
(2) A. A repairperson. B. A painter. C. An exterminator. D. A plumber.	
(3) A. It's on the third floor. B. It's in bad condition. C. It's in a good neighborhood. D. It's cheap.	

PART **II** Reading

Section 1　Pre-reading Activity

1. Directions: *The passage you are going to read talks about "vocational education". In groups, discuss the importance of vocational education and answer the following questions.*

(1) What is vocational education?

(2) How does vocational education differ from traditional academic education?

(3) What are the key goals of vocational education?

2. Directions: *The following are a few lines from the passage. In your opinion, what are they talking about?*

(1) "My country wants to cultivate well-skilled human capital for industry..."

(2) "Advancing the BRI increased the need for Luban Workshops..."

(3) "Development of e-commerce and the digital economy are the priorities for Rwanda's Vision 2050."

(4) "The training provides comprehensive knowledge, interactive sessions and valuable hands-on experience..."

Developing Nations Benefit from Chinese Expertise[①]

Adson Hak, who comes from **Ethiopia**, spent most of his time last year in a Chinese laboratory **fine-tuning** his skills in using industrial robots. He enrolled at Tianjin University of Technology and Education in 2019 for training in intelligent **manufacturing** and automation, as part of programs launched by China to help African countries improve the skills of their **workforces**.

His desire to put what he learned into practice increased after the university established a Luban **Workshop** in Ethiopia in 2021. The workshop was part of the professional training programs offered by China's **vocational** education colleges with the aim of sharing **expertise**.

"My country wants to cultivate well-skilled human capital for industry, especially in the private sector in Ethiopia and throughout East Africa. My mission is to be the best teacher returning home to pass on the knowledge I acquired in China," he said. Like many African nations, the vocational education system in Ethiopia is still in its **infancy**, and sharing experience from China is vital to enable the transfer of technologies to small and micro businesses, he added.

To date, Chinese colleges have established 11 Luban Workshops in African countries, offering a wide range of professional training and help for the younger generation in these nations to build up their professional skills. Named after Lu Ban, an ancient Chinese **woodcraft** master, the workshops have risen in popularity in recent years to become a **centerpiece** of the drive by Beijing to promote international cooperation on vocational education.

Liu Bin, President of the Alliance for the Development of Luban Workshops, said a

---

① From *China Daily*.

crucial factor behind the **flourishing** vocational training programs is that they seek to meet the **surging** demand for improved local labor forces as Chinese businesses and products become globalized. A total of 27 Luban Workshops have been established in 25 countries, most of which are in developing countries. The programs provide training in vocational skills **tailored** to meet the demands of the host countries.

Another crucial factor **underpinning** the popularity of the workshops is the deepening cooperation between China and countries taking part in the Belt and Road Initiative, or BRI. "Advancing the BRI increased the need for the Luban Workshops, which has also given **impetus** to the initiative," Liu said.

Most of the workshops are located at vocational colleges in host countries, and they are usually established through **partnerships** between such colleges in China and their local **counterparts**. The Chinese institutions share their equipments, teaching methods and materials, and provide training for the teachers.

Since the first Luban Workshop outside China was set up in Thailand in 2016, the 27 workshops established to date offer degrees to more than 6,100 students and temporary training programs for some 31,500 students. Liu said the workshops have also provided training for more than 4,000 teachers from host countries.

Some African nations have already benefited from the vocational education cooperation programs. In Djibouti, the first 24 students trained by a Luban Workshop in fields, such as railway operations and rail engineering technology, have become **interns** for the Addis Ababa-Djibouti Railway.

The workshop, which is the first of its kind **launched** by China in Africa, is expected to help train talent, which is in short supply, to ensure the **maintenance** and operations of the railway, a **flagship** BRI project built by Chinese construction companies.

In Rwanda, a Luban Workshop jointly established by China's Jinhua **Polytechnic** and the Integrated Polytechnic Regional College Musanze, or IPRC Musanze, offers students training in skills such as **telecommunications**, smart manufacturing, electrical automation technology and e-commerce.

Xu Tengfei, head of the international exchanges department at Jinhua Polytechnic in Jinhua, Zhejiang province, said that the workshop has offered more than 9,000 training **sessions** for students from the African nation. "Development of e-commerce and the digital economy are the priorities for Rwanda's Vision 2050. This is why we offer training in these two sectors," Xu said.

Ezra Muremi, **Deputy** Principal of IPRC Musanze, said the training provided by the Luban Workshop is highly regarded, with participants expressing gratitude for the chance to enhance their skills. "The training provides comprehensive knowledge, interactive sessions and valuable **hands-on** experience, contributing to participants' confidence in applying their new skills to improve their work performance and support organizational growth," he said.

A crucial factor behind the popularity of Luban Workshops is the strong expertise from China's vocational education system, based on the nation's **robust** manufacturing and services sectors. **Executives** from many Chinese vocational colleges said the majors established at Luban Workshops are those that the colleges have the strongest expertise in.

Xu said Jinhua's **booming** e-commerce sector has long been a strong **pillar** for the college to strengthen its e-commerce majors. "In cooperating with our counterparts in Rwanda, we share our best resources and try to cater to their urgent requirements for professional training," he added.

(801 words)

 ## New Words

Ethiopia	/ˌiːθiˈəʊpiə/	*n.*	埃塞俄比亚
fine-tune	/ˌfaɪn ˈtjuːn/	*v.*	微调
manufacture	/ˌmænjuˈfæktʃə/	*v./n.*	生产
workforce	/ˈwɜːkfɔːs/	*n.*	劳动力；雇员总数
workshop	/ˈwɜːkʃɒp/	*n.*	讨论会；车间
vocational	/vəʊˈkeɪʃən(ə)l/	*adj.*	职业的
expertise	/ˌekspɜːˈtiːz/	*n.*	专业技能；专业知识
infancy	/ˈɪnfənsi/	*n.*	婴儿期
woodcraft	/ˈwʊdˌkraːft/	*n.*	木工技术
centerpiece	/ˈsentəpiːs/	*n.*	中心装饰品；核心
flourish	/ˈflʌrɪʃ/	*v.*	繁荣；兴旺
surge	/sɜːdʒ/	*v./n.*	剧增；涌动
tailor	/ˈteɪlə/	*n.*	裁缝
		v.	调整
underpin	/ˌʌndəˈpɪn/	*v.*	支撑；加固
impetus	/ˈɪmpɪtəs/	*n.*	推动力；促进因素
partnership	/ˈpɑːtnəʃɪp/	*n.*	伙伴关系
counterpart	/ˈkaʊntəpɑːt/	*n.*	对应的人或物

intern	/ɪn'tɜːn/	n.	实习生；实习医生
launch	/lɔːntʃ/	v./n.	发起
maintenance	/'meɪntənəns/	n.	检修；维持
flagship	/'flægʃɪp/	n.	王牌产品；旗舰
polytechnic	/ˌpɒli'teknɪk/	n.	理工院校
telecommunication	/ˌtelikəˌmjuːnɪ'keɪʃ(ə)n/	n.	电信
session	/'seʃ(ə)n/	n.	会议；（一场）活动
deputy	/'depjuti/	n.	副手
hands-on	/ˌhændz 'ɒn/	adj.	亲身实践的
robust	/rəʊ'bʌst/	adj.	健壮的；强有力的
executive	/ɪg'zekjətɪv/	n.	执行总监
		adj.	执行的
boom	/buːm/	n.	繁荣
		v.	激增
pillar	/'pɪlə/	n.	柱子

Phrases and Expressions

pass on	传给
be in its infancy	处于初级阶段
to date	迄今
build up	建立；使逐渐变大
name sb./sth. after sb./sth.	以……命名
give rise to	造成；引起
in short supply	供应不足
cater to sb./sth	迎合；满足……的需要

Section 2   Reading Comprehension

1. Directions: *Read the passage as quickly as you can. Answer the questions.*

(1) Where did Adson Hak spend most of his time last year?

(2) When was the Luban Workshop established in Ethiopia?

(3) How many Luban Workshops have been established in African countries to date?

(4) Which railway project in Djibouti has benefited from the vocational education cooperation programs?

(5) Which goals of vocational education from your discussion in Pre-reading Activity 1 are mentioned?

2. Directions: *Read the passage again. Decide whether the following statements are true (T) or false (F).*

(1) Adson Hak enrolled at Tianjin University of Technology and Education in 2019.

(   )

(2) The Luban Workshop in Ethiopia was the first one established by China in Africa.

(   )

(3) The workshops offer tailored vocational skills training for the host countries. (   )

(4) The popularity of the workshops is primarily due to the demand for improved labor forces in China.

(   )

(5) Chinese colleges are solely responsible for the establishment of Luban Workshops in African countries.

(   )

(6) The training provided by the workshop includes interactive sessions and hands-on experience.

(   )

(7) The majors established at Luban Workshops are unrelated to the expertise of Chinese vocational colleges.

(   )

(8) Jinhua Polytechnic benefits from Rwanda's booming e-commerce sector to strengthen its e-commerce programs.

(   )

What Do You Think?

3. Directions: *Discuss the followings in small groups or pairs. Then report to the class.*

(1) In what ways can vocational education initiatives, like the establishment of Luban Workshops, contribute to fostering entrepreneurship, innovation, and economic development in developing countries beyond their immediate impact on workforce skills?

(2) Explore the potential challenges and opportunities for promoting vocational education in rural areas or regions with limited resources. How can technology and digital platforms be leveraged to overcome these barriers and make vocational education more accessible?

(3) Discuss the significance of lifelong learning in the context of vocational education. How can educational systems encourage individuals to embrace continuous learning and upskilling throughout their careers to adapt to evolving technological advancements and job market requirements?

(4) Compare and contrast vocational education systems across different countries. What can be learned from successful models of vocational education in countries like China and Germany, and how can these insights be applied to benefit other nations?

(5) Examine the potential impact of vocational education programs in reducing youth unemployment rates and fostering social and economic mobility. How can governments and stakeholders collaborate to ensure that vocational education becomes a viable and attractive choice for young individuals?

(6) Reflect on the future of vocational education and its role in preparing individuals for the jobs of tomorrow. What skills should vocational education programs prioritize to adapt to emerging industries, automation, and the changing nature of work?

Vocabulary

4. Directions: Read the following sentences. Search the passage for words that mean the same as those underlined.

(1) He spent hours **adjusting and refining** his guitar to achieve the perfect tone before his performance.

(2) The company experienced a **sharp increase** in sales after launching their new product.

(3) The CEO of the company met with her overseas **equivalent** to discuss potential areas of collaboration and exchange ideas.

(4) A strong educational foundation **is the backbone of** a person's ability to succeed in their chosen field.

(5) Regular **caring and servicing** of the equipment is essential to ensure its optimal performance and longevity.

5. Directions: Complete the following sentences with the correct form of words from the passage.

(1) With the right training and development programs, companies can empower their w _____ to reach their full potential.

(2) When science was in its **i** _____, the Greeks believed that the Earth was at the centre of the universe.

(3) Our company offers a range of services that can be **t** _____ to meet the specific requirements of each client.

(4) The recent surge in renewable energy investments has provided a significant **i** _____ for the development of clean and sustainable technologies.

(5) During his **i** _____ship, John had the opportunity to learn from experienced professionals and contribute to real projects within the company.

(6) The science class provides students with **h** _____ opportunities to conduct experiments and engage in practical learning.

(7) Members will encourage more schools to embrace a rigorous curriculum, including regular testing, longer school days and a **r** _____ approach to behaviour.

(8) Public transport has not been able to cope adequately with the travel **b** _____.

6. Directions: *Complete the following sentences by selecting suitable phrases in the box.*

pass on	be in its infancy	to date	build up
name sb./sth. after sb./sth.	give rise to	in short supply	cater to sb./sth.

(1) The scientific discoveries in the field of medicine _____ breakthrough treatments and therapies, revolutionizing the way diseases are treated and improving patient outcomes.

(2) Our team has achieved remarkable results in the project, delivering the best performance _____.

(3) She told us about his brother, Apollo, born in 1969 and _____ the US astronauts' mission to the moon.

(4) Sometimes it is simply employing inexperienced or inept workers when skilled labour is _____.

(5) William Tell, director of education for Crunch Fitness, said the global gym chain has shuffled its spaces to better _____ its members' interests.

PART **III** Understanding Global Issues

 Strategies for Better Speaking

Speaking Skill: Interpreting Information in Tables and Charts

Tables and charts are often used in reports and presentations as they can tell clearly and vividly information involving a series of numbers. Besides, they can show the relations among the data visually. When interpreting message in tables and charts, attention should be given to **title, source, description of change and tendency, interpretation.** The following sentence patterns are for your reference:

1) Title: This table/ bar-chart of...

2) Source: The data are collected from... by...

3) Description of change and tendency: The year... witnessed a soar in..., The sales saw a slight/sharp decrease in...

4) Interpretation: The sharp increase in the previous... years may result from/in... The contrast between the two may be the reason of... A mild prediction can be made...

Exercise

Directions: *PISA (Programme for International Student Assessment) is the OECD's Program for International Student Assessment. It measures 15-year-olds' ability to use their reading, mathematics and science knowledge and skills to meet real-life challenges. Read the following information and work with your partner to come up with a 3-minute story that features the topic of education, following the seven steps below. Please also refer to the four questions at the bottom as your prompts.*

Table 1　Numbers of PISA Items by Domain and Across Cycles in the Main Survey

	2000	2003	2006	2009	2012	2015	2018
Reading	129	28	28	131	44	103	245
Mathematics	43	84	48	35	109	83	83
Science	45	34	103	53	53	184	115

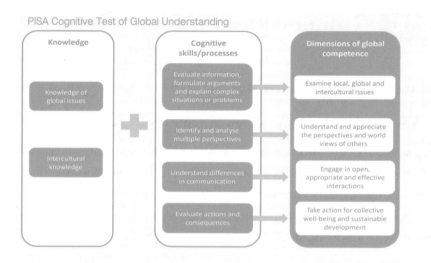

Figure 1   The Relationship Between the Cognitive Test of Global Understanding and the Dimensions of Global Competence

Step 1: Read Table 1 and Figure 1, brainstorm with your partner and decide a specific perspective to explore the topic.

Step 2: Search the Internet for more information on PISA.

Step 3: Interpret Table 1 and Figure 1 with strategies learned above/in the Speaking Skill Section.

Step 4: Weave the interpretation into the story, and use as many words as you can from Part I and Part II.

Step 5: Tell your partner the story, and switch roles when you finish.

Step 6: Work together to polish the more interesting story.

Step 7: Be prepared to share your story in front of the whole class.

(1) What is the role of education in shaping the future for mankind?

(2) In your opinion, what are the most significant challenges that our education system faces today?

(3) What are some potential solutions to ensure equal opportunities for all students?

(4) What are some global educational issues that require collective action, and how can we contribute to addressing them?

(5) Are students ready to thrive in an interconnected world?

Unit 3

Innovation

PART Ⅰ Listening and Speaking

Section 1 Pre-listening Activity

Directions: Browse the questions below and discuss one of the following questions with your partner. List the key information, and share your opinion with the class.

(1) Can you describe a creative solution you've developed to tackle a challenge?

(2) What innovative methods or applications have you encountered in your life?

(3) Can you describe four significant innovations in the Chinese history?

(4) Can you describe the most significant innovation in the world?

(5) What do you consider to be the most significant innovation in the world and why?

(6) What revolutions is AI expected to bring to humanity?

Section 2 Listening Comprehension

Passage One

Directions: Listen to the passage. Choose the best answer to each question.

(1) Intelligent connected buses hit the road in Chongqing for a _____.

    A. task   B. test

    C. competition   D. show

(2) These commuting buses are _____.

    A. manned vehicles

    B. part of the cloud-controlled infrastructure

    C. autonomous demonstration

    D. conventional applications

(3) The operation of these buses is based on the following technological solutions except _____.

    A. the vehicles   B. the road

    C. the cloud platform   D. traffic lights

(4) The "driving instructor" gives real-time advice to vehicles so that they could facilitate the drive _____.

A. faster

B. safer

C. more efficient

D. all above

(5) According to the news report, which of the following statements is true?

A. Dump trucks and five other types of vehicles have also joined the ICV demonstration zone.

B. Dump trucks and five other types of vehicles are not going to join the ICV demonstration zone.

C. Dump trucks and five other types of vehicles will also join the ICV demonstration zone.

D. Dump trucks and five other types of vehicles will join a different demonstration zone.

Passage Two

Directions: *Listen to the passage. Choose the best answer to each question.*

(1) According to the speaker, what is the paradox that the Europeans face?

A. Europeans are excellent in making money, but not so good in making science.

B. Europeans are excellent in making science, but not so good in making money.

C. Europeans are excellent in making science with money, but they are not so good in making money out of science.

D. Europeans are excellent in making money with science, but they are not so good in making science out of money.

(2) Which of the following statements is ***NOT*** true?

A. The European Innovation Council will fund small-and medium-size companies with high potential.

B. The European Innovation Council will not fund small-and medium-size companies with high risks.

C. The European Innovation Council will support innovative researchers that have ideas for the next breakthrough technology.

D. The European Innovation Council will offer coaching to support entrepreneurs to set up a business.

(3) In this year, half of the money will be given to support _____.

    A. the Green Deal

    B. digital technologies

    C. health innovation

    D. all above

(4) It can be inferred from the speech that CorWave _____.

    A. is one of the first companies to receive venture capital from the Commission

    B. is good to patients who have heart failure

    C. is an innovative company that does clinical tests

    D. sells ideas to make money from the market

(5) The European Innovation Council _____.

    A. will support top researchers based on scientific excellence

    B. is a branch of the European Research Council

    C. will support breakthrough technology and scale up disruptive innovation

    D. has completed innovation in Europe

Strategies for Better Listening

Listening Skill: Getting Meaning from Context—Prediction

In listening, active listeners usually predict what they're going to get based on what's already been heard. Transitional words functioning as coherence and cohesion often serve as signals within a sentence or among sentences, telling the listeners the logic development of the passage or speech.

Example:

As we all know, Europe is a powerhouse in science. Our new Horizon research program is the largest ever. But we also face a big paradox: We, Europeans, are excellent in making science with money. But we are not so good in making money out of science.

Illustration:

The first "but" is a logic transition, signaling that the information in the following sentence is totally different from the "excellent" part in the previous two sentences "is a powerhouse" and "is the largest ever". The second "but" makes it clear again that "the Europeans are excellent in making science with money but not so good in making money out of science", which is something contradictory, thus regarded as a paradox.

Exercise

Directions: *Listen to Passage Two again and put down more examples from the speech with signal words of "but" and "also". Then explain the logical development with the help of those transitions.*

(1) _____

(2) _____

(3) _____

PART　Ⅱ　Reading

Section 1　Pre-reading Activity

1. Directions: *The passage you are going to read talks about "agricultural drones". In groups, discuss the use of drones in agriculture and answer the following questions.*

(1) What do you know about agricultural drones?

(2) What are some of the challenges faced by farmers in traditional agriculture methods?

(3) How do you think advanced technologies like agricultural drones can benefit the agricultural sector?

2. Directions: *The following are a few lines from the passage. In your opinion, what are they talking about?*

(1) "... local farmers often face a heavy financial burden and low profit margins."

(2) "A shortage of agricultural labor has become a long-term problem for many countries..."

(3) "... provided free plant protection services so they could familiarize themselves with the new technology."

(4) "The degree to which agricultural drones are accepted in overseas markets depends on local laws and regulations as well as farmers' awareness of new technologies."

Agricultural Drone Makers Eye Overseas Markets[①]

Entrepreneur Ma Zhiqiang is introducing **innovative** Chinese technologies, including agricultural **drones**, to **Ecuador**, a South American nation known for its crops such as bananas, cocoa and coffee. Ma, who used to work as a technician for a Chinese medical equipment company, was sent to Ecuador for eight months in 1982 as part of his duties. Attracted by the nation's beautiful and diverse landscape, after returning home to China, he quit his job and returned to Ecuador to start a business.

Born in a farming family, Ma has a strong feeling for the land, and started a farm to grow rice, cocoa and mangoes. Due to a shortage of smart agricultural equipment, most farmers in Ecuador still relied on **manpower** to seed, fertilize and spray **pesticides** on their land.

"I found that although the agricultural economy in Ecuador is developed, local farmers often face a heavy financial burden and low profit **margins**. They are in great need of efficient and precision equipment such as drones to improve working efficiency," Ma said.

"Chinese agricultural drones have taken the lead in high-precision **navigation** and spraying, so I wanted to introduce **cutting-edge** Chinese technologies and products to Ecuador," Ma added, noting that fully automated drones are ideal on banana plantations.

Compared with traditional manual spraying and fixed-wing aircraft, such drones have **intricate** technology to accurately control **droplet** size, flow rate and spray area. With a powerful **downdraft**, **minute** droplets are spread evenly on crop leaves, reducing chemical **drift** to safely minimize environmental contamination.

After careful analysis and comparison, Ma finally chose devices developed by XAG, China's largest agricultural drone manufacturer. "My team and I initially bought several drones to demonstrate the spraying effect to local farmers. We even provided free plant protection services so they could familiarize themselves with the new technology. We also attended large agricultural exhibitions, trade fairs and academic forums to promote farm drones," Ma said.

His company, Megadrone SA, has collaborated with Dole, one of the world's largest producers and **distributors** of high-quality fresh fruit, and with German life sciences company Bayer. It also offers drone pilot training courses to create employment opportunities for young people in rural areas.

---

① From *China Daily*.

"Next, we plan to establish a long-term cooperation **mechanism** with local governments and educational institutions in Ecuador to promote drone technology and equipment through schools and other institutions," Ma said. His company has business partners in Brazil and Chile. Potential customers have also **emerged** in Colombia and Argentina, and he hopes to provide quality services to more **clients** in South America.

With the modernization of agriculture, demand for advanced farming devices has grown significantly. According to the experts, agricultural drones are widely used for **sowing** seeds and spraying fertilizers and pesticides, increasing the efficiency and management of plant protection and grain production.

Justin Gong, co-founder of XAG, said: "A shortage of agricultural labor has become a long-term problem for many countries, which are making stronger demands for **autonomous** drones and robots. We hope to bring more **unmanned** farming devices to overseas markets through working with local partners and distributors."

Gong said that farmers in Brazil, Ecuador, Chile and other South American countries with complex **terrain** attach more importance to the flexibility and precision of spraying, and farm drones are mainly used in banana, cocoa, coffee and sugar **cane** plantations. "In the next few years, we expect agricultural drones to be used on a larger scale in Southeast Asia, Eastern Europe and South America," Gong added.

He said XAG, which is based in Guangzhou, capital of Guangdong province, will step up efforts to expand its presence in Ukraine and Brazil—two major grain producing areas. The company is also looking for opportunities in Southeast Asia and in Japan and South Korea, which have solid foundations for agricultural **machinery**.

"We are confident of bringing mature products and solutions to overseas markets and of improving agricultural production efficiency worldwide," Gong said. He added that XAG's overseas sales have grown rapidly despite the COVID-19 **pandemic**, and will gradually become an important part of the company's overall **revenue**.

The degree to which agricultural drones are accepted in overseas markets depends on local laws and regulations as well as farmers' awareness of new technologies. XAG is carrying out technology promotion, education and drone training to cultivate more young pilots.

As of December, the company's unmanned agricultural devices had been sold in 42 countries and regions. Apart from drones, XAG has introduced farm robots in Japan, the United States, Vietnam, Thailand, the United Kingdom, Australia, Ukraine, Russia and Brazil. In June, the company's R150 unmanned ground vehicles made their **debut** in Japan, **pollinating** an apple **orchard** in the city of Takayama to help alleviate a labor shortage.

Civil drones comprise consumer-level and industry-level equipment. Industry experts said growth of the civil drone market is mainly coming from consumer-level devices used for aerial **photography**, but the industry-level sector will end up being worth much more.

(817 words)

 New Words

entrepreneur	/ˌɒntrəprə'nɜː/	n.	创业者
innovative	/'ɪnəˌveɪtɪv/	adj.	创新的；富有创新精神的
drone	/drəʊn/	n.	无人驾驶飞机
Ecuador	/'ekwədɔːr/	n.	厄瓜多尔
manpower	/'mænˌpaʊə/	n.	劳动力
pesticide	/'pestɪˌsaɪd/	n.	杀虫剂
margin	/'mɑːdʒɪn/	n.	盈余；边缘
navigation	/ˌnævɪ'geɪʃən/	n.	航行；导航
cutting-edge	/ˌkʌtɪŋ 'edʒ/	adj.	尖端的
intricate	/'ɪntrɪkɪt/	adj.	复杂精细的
droplet	/'drɒplɪt/	n.	小滴
downdraft	/'daʊndrɑːft/	n.	向下之气流或风
minute	/maɪ'njuːt/	adj.	微小的；非常小的
drift	/drɪft/	n.	移动
distributor	/dɪ'strɪbjʊtə/	n.	经销商
mechanism	/'mekəˌnɪzəm/	n.	机制
emerge	/ɪ'mɜːdʒ/	v.	出现，浮现
client	/'klaɪənt/	n.	客户
sow	/səʊ/	v.	播种
autonomous	/ɔː'tɒnəməs/	adj.	自主的；自治的
unmanned	/ʌn'mænd/	adj.	无人驾驶的
terrain	/tə'reɪn/	n.	地形
cane	/keɪn/	n.	（竹或甘蔗的）茎；手杖
machinery	/mə'ʃiːnərɪ/	n.	机器；机械

pandemic	/pæn'demɪk/	n.	流行病
revenue	/'revɪˌnjuː/	n.	（公司或政府等的）收入
debut	/'deɪbjuː/	n.	首次登台
pollinate	/'pɒlɪˌneɪt/	v.	给……传授花粉
orchard	/'ɔːtʃəd/	n.	果园
photography	/fə'tɒgrəfɪ/	n.	摄影；摄影术

Phrases and Expressions

start a business	创业
in need of	需要……
take the lead in sth.	在某方面领先
step up	增加
carry out	实行
as of	从……开始；截至……
apart from	除了……以外
make one's debut	首次亮相

Section 2　Reading Comprehension

1. Directions: Read the passage as quickly as you can. Answer the questions.

(1) Who is Ma Zhiqiang?

(2) In which country are efforts being made to introduce Chinese agricultural drones?

(3) Which regions are expected to see a larger-scale adoption of agricultural drones in the coming years?

(4) What potential applications of agricultural drones are mentioned in the text?

(5) Which challenges from your discussion in prereading Activity 1 are mentioned?

2. Directions: Read the passage again. Decide whether the following statements are true (T) or false (F).

(1) XAG is a Chinese company involved in the promotion of agricultural drone technology.　　　　　　　　　　　　　　　　　　　　　　　　　（　　）

(2) XAG is cooperating with local distributors and partners to expand the market for unmanned farming devices.　　　　　　　　　　　　　　　　　　（　　）

(3) XAG offers a training program exclusively for drone pilots to operate agricultural drones. ( )

(4) Agricultural drones can gather real-time data and assist in crop monitoring and yield estimation. ( )

(5) XAG's overseas sales have declined due to the COVID-19 pandemic. ( )

(6) The adoption of agricultural drones in South America is limited due to strict regulations. ( )

(7) The acceptance of agricultural drones in overseas markets is solely dependent on technological advancements. ( )

(8) XAG's R150 unmanned ground vehicles made their debut in Philippines. ( )

What Do You Think?

3. Directions: *Discuss the followings in small groups or pairs. Then report to the class.*

(1) What are some key factors that could influence the successful adoption of Chinese agricultural drones in western markets?

(2) How can Chinese drone manufacturers address concerns related to data security and privacy to gain trust and acceptance in western markets?

(3) What strategies can be employed to overcome any potential bias or skepticism towards Chinese technology in western countries?

(4) Share examples of real-world applications of agricultural drones in different farming sectors, such as crop monitoring, irrigation management, or yield estimation.

(5) What are the current regulations and policies governing the use of agricultural drones, and how do they vary across different countries?

(6) Discuss the energy efficiency and carbon footprint of agricultural drones compared with traditional farming machinery.

Vocabulary

4. Directions: *Read the following sentences. Search the passage for words that mean the same as those underlined.*

(1) Please remember to maintain a minimum one-inch **spacing** on all sides when formatting your document.

(2) Medical equipment **suppliers** said isolation gowns have emerged as the most recent vital piece of equipment in short supply.

(3) Fishing is the main industry, with seal-hunting in season serving as an additional source of **income stream**.

(4) The technology is seen as the first step towards the gradual introduction of fully **self-driving** cars that can operate themselves at higher speeds.

(5) The plot of the novel was filled with twists and turns, creating a **complex and detailed** web of suspense and intrigue.

5. Directions: *Complete the following sentences with the correct form of words from the passage.*

(1) Firms are boosting profits by finding new commercial purposes for the **u** _____ aircraft.

(2) While the reasons for the construction of these places remain unknown to us, immense resources of **m** _____ were needed to erect them.

(3) The invention of the smartphone was a groundbreaking **i** _____ that transformed the way we communicate and access information.

(4) The tourist office there can give you a map of the more mountainous **t** _____ north of town, where you can walk through wild mountain lavender.

(5) That can be done using aerial **p** _____, but it is just not economical or feasible to do on a continuous basis.

(6) Masks play an important role in preventing **d** _____ from infected individuals reaching other people.

(7) There are vineyards and cherry **o** _____ on the hillsides and the plains are planted with gorgeous fruit.

(8) The intricate details on the artwork were so **m** _____ that they required a magnifying glass to fully appreciate.

6. Directions: *Complete the following sentences by selecting suitable phrases in the box.*

start a business	in need of	take the lead	step up
carry out	as of	apart from	make one's debut

(1) The company aims to _____ in sustainable technology by developing

innovative solutions for renewable energy.

(2) _____ now, there are no available seats on the flight, but you can join the waiting list for any cancellations.

(3) Since confirming their relationship, the couple has _____ at the premiere of the final season of Idris' show Snowfall.

(4) She implored her colleagues to _____ their contributions in order to meet the fundraising goal for the charity event.

(5) Motivated by the desire for financial independence, he left his corporate job to pursue his entrepreneurial dreams and _____ in the technology sector.

PART **III** Understanding Global Issues

 Strategies for Better Speaking

Speaking Skill: Analyzing Your Audience

Audience analysis is the process of understanding who your audience will be, what their views may be, and how you can best reach them. Thoughtful audience analysis is one of the best habits you need to develop as a public speaker. It will help you discern your audience's perspective and so help you provide maximum value for them. If done well, your audience analysis will provide insights that will help you focus your message, select the most effective content and visuals, and tailor your delivery to suit this particular target audience. Study your audience in three primary dimensions:

1. **Demographic analysis** involves age, gender, culture, ethnicity, race, religion, and educational level.

2. **Attitudinal analysis** addresses the audience's attitudes, beliefs, and values.

3. **Environmental analysis** aims to find out things like the seating arrangement, the number of people likely to attend, the room lighting, and the acoustics.

Exercises

1. Directions: *Answer the five questions about your audience.*

(1) What do you and your audience have in common and how are you different?

(2) What is your audience's interest in an attitude towards your topic?

(3) What would they like to know or need to know about your topic?

(4) What ideas or examples in your speech might your audience identify with?

(5) How can your topic, or the information contained in your speech benefit your audience?

2. Directions: *Work with your partner and learn to analyze your possible target audience on the topic of innovation following the seven steps below. Please refer to the four questions below as your prompts.*

Step 1: Work together and analyze the possible audience of Listening Passage Two in this unit from the three dimensions above.

Step 2: Browse the following questions and choose one that interests you.

Step 3: Discuss with your partner and decide on the topics related to the question.

Step 4: Decide on the target audience you're to deliver the speech to.

Step 5: Analyze your audience in three steps: Demographic analysis, Attitudinal analysis, and Environmental analysis.

Step 6: Take turns to ask your partner the five specific questions above about your target audience.

Step 7: Be prepared to share your analysis with the whole class.

(1) Can you think of any examples of how innovation has addressed or could address pressing global issues, such as climate change or healthcare?

(2) How does intellectual property protection impact innovation, and how can it strike a balance between encouraging innovation and safeguarding creators' rights?

(3) How has technology-driven innovation transformed the way we live, learn, and interact with one another?

(4) How can emerging technologies like artificial intelligence, blockchain, or renewable energy shape the future of innovation?

Unit 4

Peace

PART Ⅰ Listenig and Speaking

Section 1 Pre-listening Activity

Directions: *Browse the questions below and discuss one of the following questions with your partner. List the key information, and share your opinion with the class.*

(1) Which novels or movies about wars can you recommend?

(2) What is your understanding of Benjamin Franklin's quotation, "There never was a good war or a bad peace"?

(3) Have you heard of any stories related to wars, and if so, could you share those stories?

(4) Can you discuss a war that significantly altered the course of history and explain why?

(5) What lessons can be learned from historical wars to prevent future conflicts?

(6) How can art, music, and literature contribute to a culture of peace?

Section 2 Listening Comprehension

Passage One

Directions: *Listen to the following passage. Fill in the blanks with what you hear.*

The Chinese-built Mombasa-Nairobi Standard Gauge Railway (SGR), which helps boost the (1) _____ of people, goods and services, will contribute to the long-term growth, (2) _____ and stability of the Horn of Africa region, experts have said. Speaking at a forum in Kenya's coastal city of Mombasa Wednesday, scholars from pan-African think tanks noted that since its launch on May 31, 2017, the 480-km SGR has fostered connectivity, (3) _____ trade, people-to-people interactions that boost the stability and inclusive growth of the greater Horn of Africa region. The forum, convened by Africa Policy Institute, a pan-African think tank based in Nairobi, the capital of Kenya, (4) _____ light on the centrality of the Chinese-built modern railway in promoting regional peace and development. The day-long forum, on China-Africa cooperation on the outlook on peace and development in the Horn of Africa, was held under the theme of "Kenya on (5) _____ : The Impact of the Standard Gauge Railway."

"China is deepening the structural frameworks of its (6) _____ with Horn of Africa countries. Through projects like the SGR, China has ensured that the nexus between peace and development is sustained," said Peter Kagwanja, the chief executive officer of Africa Policy Institute. The Chinese-built modern railway in Kenya reaffirms the enduring strength of mutually beneficial partnership, a key highlight of the 15th BRICS Summit in Johannesburg, South Africa, Kagwanja said.

Stephen Jackson, the UN resident coordinator for Kenya, said the SGR, a key component of the China-proposed Belt and Road (7) _____ (BRI), has demonstrated that investments in modern infrastructure have the potential to connect, prosper, and stabilize the Horn of Africa region, which has long been seen as synonymous with resource-based conflicts and climatic shocks. Thanks to unhindered trade, financial integration, improved investment climate, and enhanced human interactions facilitated by the modern railway, the region could unlock key sectors like agriculture, livestock, and (8) _____, Jackson said. He added that Chinese investments and strategic deployment of soft power have injected vitality into multilateral efforts aimed at ending strife and violent extremism in the Horn of Africa region.

The (9) _____ for long-term peace, stability, and shared growth in the region are higher, now that the Mombasa-Nairobi SGR has accelerated opening up and interconnectedness, said Mustafa Ali, chairman and co-founder of HORN International Institute for Strategic Studies, a Nairobi-based think tank. He said that Chinese-funded infrastructure projects will be key to unleashing skills and technology transfer, to empower and give hope to about 70 percent of youth in the Horn of Africa who are below 35 years of age. In addition, Ali said, Chinese investments in modern infrastructure and skills development will boost the resilience of economies in the Horn of Africa, helping prevent its youth from joining (10) _____ groups. The SGR has enhanced the integration of communities, a prerequisite for peace and harmony, said Fred Jonyo, the chairman of the Department of Political Science at the University of Nairobi.

Passage Two

Direction: *Listen to a passage about the history of the United Nations. Decide whether the statements are true (T) or false (F).*

(1) After World War II ended in 1945, representatives from 50 countries gathered at the United Nations Conference on International Organization in San Francisco. 　　　　　　　　　　　　　　　　　　(　)

(2) It was firmly believed that another world war like World War II could be prevented

after the United Nations was founded in 1945. ( )

(3) China was one of the countries to sign and ratify (批准，正式签署) the UN Charter.

( )

(4) Giving humanitarian assistance to those in need is one of the functions of the United Nations. ( )

(5) The Sustainable Development Goals for 2030 was part of the plan envisioned in 1945 by its founders. ( )

Strategies for Better Listening

Listening Skill: Getting Meaning from Context—Inference

With compound dictation exercises, listeners often need to get meaning from the sentences before or after the blanks, and then make inferences depending on the content information and the clue from logic development. The following example is taken from the previous listening exercise.

Example:

... since its launch on May 31, 2017, the 480-km SGR has fostered connectivity, (3) _____ trade, people-to-people interactions that boost the stability and inclusive growth of the greater Horn of Africa region.

Illustration:

The words "stability" and "inclusive growth" are the key words in the sentence, and they are the goal and positive result of the "480-km SGR" as it has fostered "connectivity, (3) _____ trade, people-to-people interactions", from abstract to specific.

Exercise

Directions: Read the following sentences on peace. Fill in the blanks with the help of the context.

(1) In a world rife with conflicts and disputes, achieving lasting _____ remains a paramount goal for global leaders. They gather at summits and engage in _____ negotiations to find ways to preserve harmony among nations.

(2) The leaders of neighboring countries held _____ talks, aiming to find common ground and build trust for a peaceful coexistence along their shared border.

(3) In a world where divisions and mistrust seem to prevail, initiatives promoting cultural _____ and understanding are more important than ever. Such efforts can foster a sense of unity and contribute to a more _____ world.

(4) International organizations work tirelessly to address the root causes of conflicts and promote _____ through diplomacy and humanitarian efforts. Their goal is to create a world where all people can live in _____.

PART II   Reading

Section 1   Pre-reading Activity

1. Directions: *The passage you are going to read talks about "peaceful development". In groups, discuss the following questions.*

(1) What does "peaceful development" mean in the context of China's foreign policy?

(2) How does China's Belt and Road Initiative (BRI) align with its strategy of peaceful development?

(3) How do other countries perceive China's path of peaceful development?

2. Directions: *The following are a few lines from the passage. In your opinion, what are they talking about?*

(1) "... the global landscape is experiencing rapid changes unseen in a century..."

(2) "... insisting on mutual benefits and win-win outcomes instead of zero-sum games."

(3) "Beijing strengthens its overseas security capabilities and guards against systemic security risks..."

(4) "China will increase cooperation with other developing countries to safeguard the common interests of developing countries..."

Peaceful Development Prioritized in Chinese Path to Modernization①

China is **fostering amicable** relations with its neighbors, while **upholding** an independent and peaceful foreign policy. Pursuing a path of peaceful development,

① From CGTN.

promoting the creation of a shared future for **humanity**, and **forging** a new model for human advancement are the vital demands, **inevitable** choices, and distinct features of the Chinese path to modernization.

Currently, the global **landscape** is experiencing rapid changes unseen in a century, with the changes of the world, of our times and of history **looming** large. **Amid** this global transformation, China's **diplomacy** is forging ahead to defend the country's **sovereignty**, security and developmental interests, while promoting a new type of international relations, and participating in the reform and building of the global governance system.

Meanwhile, China stands firm against all forms of **hegemonism**, power politics, cold war mentality, interference in other nations' internal affairs, and double standards. With composure and confidence in the **realm** of competition among major countries, China has taken hard-earned **strides** to **tackle** numerous severe risks and challenges. China adheres to peaceful development, playing a constructive role.

In the current complex of an ever-changing world, China's diplomatic achievements lie in the following aspects: China adheres to the diplomatic principles of peace, development, cooperation, and win-win outcomes, while **safeguarding** world peace and promoting common development, standing on the right side of history and human progress.

Based on human development trends, the changing global landscape and China's development throughout history, Beijing's diplomacy recognizes and handles its relationship with the outside world, upholding international fairness and justice, and insisting on mutual benefits and win-win outcomes instead of **zero-sum games**. China upholds fairness and justice and acts as a builder of world peace, contributor to global development, and defender of international order. China's development strengthens the global forces for peace.

This can be proved by the recently issued Joint **Trilateral** Statement by the People's Republic of China, the Kingdom of Saudi Arabia, and the Islamic Republic of Iran, which says that Saudi Arabia and Iran have agreed to **restore** diplomatic relations and reopen their **embassies** and missions within two months of the China-mediated talks in Beijing.

Besides, China pursues a **holistic** approach to national security and upholds independence, self-reliance and self-improvement. Through promoting international security, China ensures that both internal and external security, homeland and public security, traditional and non-traditional security, and China's own and common security. Beijing strengthens its overseas security capabilities and guards against systemic security risks, by not yielding an inch on matters of principle.

China takes a coordinated approach to safeguard and shape national security and upgrading the mechanisms for participation in global security. China is creating a new development **paradigm** underpinned by a new security paradigm and joins hands with other countries to address various global challenges. China stresses reliance on its efforts to drive the nation's development, and keep the fate of its development and progress firmly in its own hands.

Moreover, China promotes the common values of all humanity, including peace, development, fairness, justice, democracy and freedom. China respects the diversity of world civilizations and promotes cultural exchanges and mutual learning, and believes that cultural exchanges can transcend **estrangement**; mutual learning can **transcend** clashes; and **coexistence** can transcend feelings of **superiority**.

China will increase cooperation with other developing countries to safeguard the common interests of developing countries, and provides new opportunities for the world through its own new development, pushing forward the construction of a better world.

2023 marked the beginning of building a modern socialist country and advancing the great **rejuvenation** of the Chinese nation along Chinese path to modernization. China's diplomacy with Chinese characteristics for a new era faces new opportunities and challenges, and is destined to achieve new progress and accomplishments.

Xi Jinping Thought on Diplomacy is a crucial component of Xi Jinping Thought on Socialism with Chinese Characteristics for a New Era. It represents a major theoretical achievement that combines Marxist basic principles with China's distinctive diplomatic practices, while serving as an action plan for China's foreign policy in the new era.

To advance the diplomacy with Chinese characteristics in the new era, we must adhere to Xi Jinping Thought on Diplomacy and use its principles, viewpoints and methods. We should stick to the peaceful development path and win-win cooperation. It's also essential to uphold China's positions, keep in mind both domestic and international **imperatives**, and build a new pattern of relationship between great powers, featuring peaceful coexistence, overall stability and balanced development.

It's necessary to advance Chinese studies in the new **era**, **expedite** a Chinese **discourse** and **narrative** systems, tell China's stories, spread China's voice, enhance the **dissemination** and influence of Chinese civilization, promote Chinese culture's global **outreach**, and forge a new paradigm of China's diplomacy with Chinese characteristics in the new era.

(788 words)

New Words

foster	/ˈfɒstə/	v.	促进
amicable	/ˈæmɪkəbəl/	adj.	友好的
uphold	/ʌpˈhəʊld/	v.	坚持；维护
forge	/fɔːdʒ/	v.	努力缔造
inevitable	/ɪnˈevɪtəbəl/	adj.	必然发生的
landscape	/ˈlændˌskeɪp/	n.	风景；局面
loom	/luːm/	v.	可能发生；逐渐逼近
amid	/əˈmɪd/	prep.	在……当中
diplomacy	/dɪˈpləʊməsɪ/	n.	外交
sovereignty	/ˈsɒvrəntɪ/	n.	主权
hegemonism	/hiːˈgemənɪzəm/	n.	霸权主义
realm	/relm/	n.	（活动、思想的）领域
stride	/straɪd/	n.	大步
		v.	大步走
tackle	/ˈtækəl/	v.	处理；攻击
safeguard	/ˈseɪfˌgaːd/	v.	保护；保卫
trilateral	/traɪˈlætərəl/	adj.	三边的
embassy	/ˈembəsɪ/	n.	大使馆；大使及其随员
holistic	/həʊˈlɪstɪk/	adj.	整体的；全面的
paradigm	/ˈpærəˌdaɪm/	n.	范例
estrangement	/ɪˈstreɪndʒmənt/	n.	疏远；失和
transcend	/trænˈsend/	v.	超越
superiority	/suːˌpɪərɪˈɒrɪtɪ/	n.	优势
rejuvenation	/rɪˌdʒuːvəˈneɪʃn/	n.	恢复活力；振兴
imperative	/ɪmˈperətɪv/	adj.	至关重要的
		n.	紧迫之事
era	/ˈɪərə/	n.	时代
expedite	/ˈekspɪˌdaɪt/	v.	加快
discourse	/ˈdɪskɔːs/	n.	话语；会话
narrative	/ˈnærətɪv/	n.	故事；叙事
dissemination	/dɪˌsemɪˈneɪʃ(ə)n/	n.	宣传；散播
outreach	/ˈaʊtriːtʃ/	n.	外展服务；主动帮助

Phrases and Expressions

forge ahead	继续推进
stand against	公开反对某事或某人
adhere to	遵守；坚持
zero-sum game	零和游戏
push forward	推进
stick to	紧跟；坚持

Section 2　Reading Comprehension

1. Directions: Read the passage as quickly as you can. Answer the questions.

(1) What are the four diplomatic principles that China adheres to?

(2) Which three countries are involved in the Joint Trilateral Statement?

(3) What kind of approach does China take to its national security?

(4) What common values of humanity does China promote?

(5) Does the text mention a particular year that signifies an important milestone in China's development and diplomatic efforts?

2. Directions: Read the passage again. Decide whether the following statements are true (T) or false (F).

(1) China is currently experiencing changes in the global landscape that are unprecedented in a century.　　　　　　　　　　　　　　　　　　　(　　)

(2) China stands firm against all forms of hegemonism, power politics, and interference in other nations' internal affairs.　　　　　　　　　　　　　　(　　)

(3) China's approach to national security does not consider traditional security matters.　　　　　　　　　　　　　　　　　　　　　　　　　　(　　)

(4) China believes that cultural exchanges lead to feelings of superiority.　(　　)

(5) China promotes cultural exchanges and mutual learning to transcend estrangement and clashes among civilizations.　　　　　　　　　　　　　(　　)

(6) China aims to tell its own stories and spread its voice globally as mentioned in the text.　　　　　　　　　　　　　　　　　　　　　　　　(　　)

(7) The passage emphasizes the need for China to minimize its influence on the global stage.　　　　　　　　　　　　　　　　　　　　　　　　　(　　)

(8) According to the passage, China's goal is to construct a better world by providing new opportunities through its own development.   (   )

What Do You Think?

3. Directions: *Discuss the followings in small groups or pairs. Then report to the class.*

(1) In what ways is China actively participating in the reform and building of the global governance system? How does it aim to contribute to a new type of international relations, and what challenges might it face in this pursuit?

(2) The text mentions China's opposition to hegemonism and power politics. How does China's foreign policy reflect this stance, and what strategies does China employ to maintain its sovereignty and security while advocating for a peaceful and cooperative global order?

(3) How does China's holistic approach to national security, as described in the text, differ from traditional security paradigms? What are the potential benefits and drawbacks of this approach, both for China and for the global security landscape?

(4) How does China's increased cooperation with other developing countries contribute to safeguarding their common interests? What potential benefits can this cooperation bring to the world, and how does it align with China's own development goals?

(5) How do the promotion and dissemination of Chinese culture contribute to forging a new paradigm of China's diplomacy in the new era? What role does enhancing the influence of Chinese civilization play in China's diplomatic goals and its image on the global stage?

(6) How does China balance its domestic imperatives with its international commitments in its diplomatic approach? What are the potential opportunities and challenges in keeping both perspectives in mind while advancing China's diplomacy with Chinese characteristics?

Vocabulary

4. Directions: *Read the following sentences. Search the passsage for words that mean the same as those underlined.*

(1) Change is a fact of life that **cannot be avoided**; it is a constant force that shapes our experiences and challenges us to adapt and grow.

(2) The history of colonialism is often seen as a manifestation of **dominating ambitions**, as powerful nations sought to expand their influence and assert control over weaker territories.

(3) After years of unresolved conflicts and misunderstandings, the **emotional distance** between the two siblings had become insurmountable.

(4) The newly implemented urban renewal project aims to bring **new life and revitalization** to the city's neglected neighborhoods, rejuvenating the community and attracting investments.

(5) Social media platforms have played a significant role in the rapid **spread or sharing** of news and information around the world.

5. Directions: *Complete the following sentences with the correct form of words from the passage.*

(1) Despite facing numerous setbacks, the entrepreneur managed to **f** _____ a successful startup company.

(2) As we drove through the countryside, we marveled at the diverse **l** _____, from serene lakes to rugged mountains.

(3) International law recognizes the principle of **s** _____ as a core element of the state's legal existence.

(4) It is crucial for healthcare professionals to practice proper hygiene protocols to **s** _____ patients from potential infections.

(5) By embracing innovation and change, organizations can create new **p** _____ for success.

(6) Music has the unique ability to **t** _____ boundaries and unite people from diverse backgrounds through its universal language of melody and rhythm.

(7) A well-organized transportation system can significantly **e** _____ the delivery of goods and services.

(8) The film's nonlinear **n** _____ structure added an element of suspense and kept the audience engaged throughout.

6. Directions: *Complete the following sentences by selecting suitable phrases in the box.*

| forge ahead | stand against | adhere to |
| zero-sum game | push forward | stick to |

(1) Negotiations can become challenging when parties approach it as a _____,

focusing solely on winning at the expense of others.

(2) As a responsible citizen, it is crucial to _____ traffic rules and regulations for the safety of oneself and others.

(3) Despite the challenges posed by the pandemic, the school community came together to support one another and _____ with remote learning initiatives.

(4) The community united to _____ environmental degradation and raise awareness about the importance of conservation.

PART **III** Understanding Global Issues

Strategies for Better Speaking

Speaking Skill: Outlining a Speech

Using an outline to help with the preparation of a speech ensures a clear structure thus facilitates the audience's comprehension.

I. Introduction

1. Opener: General statements introducing the topic often take forms of quotations, stories, questions, and personal experiences

2. Thesis: Main point or opinion of the speech, and possible subtopics

II. Body

1. First subtopic: Topic and controlling idea

1) First detail/example/argument about subtopic A

2) Second detail/example/argument

3) ...

2. Second subtopic: Topic and controlling idea

3. ...

III. Conclusion

1. A brief summary of the main points

2. Concluding sentence: an opinion, a solution, a prediction

Exercise

Directions: *Work with your partner and come up with a 3-minute story that features the topic of peace, following the seven steps below. Please also refer to the four questions below as your prompts.*

Step 1: Browse the following questions and choose those interest you.

Step 2: Discuss with your partner and decide on the main topic and subtopics.

Step 3: Come up with an outline following the framework above.

Step 4: Add specific information or evidence as the detail.

Step 5: Check if conclusion echoes main thesis in the introduction.

Step 6: Take turns to deliver the speech to check comprehension.

Step 7: Rehearse and be prepared to share the speech with the whole class.

(1) How do you define "peace", and why is it essential for the well-being of nations and the world as a whole?

(2) Can you discuss some of the major challenges and obstacles to achieving and maintaining global peace in today's world?

(3) In your opinion, what role do international cooperation and organizations like the United Nations play in promoting and maintaining peace?

(4) How has the concept of "soft power" evolved in the context of international relations, and how does it contribute to peace efforts?

Unit 5

Justice

PART **I** Listening and Speaking

Section 1 Pre-listening Activity

Directions: Browse the questions below and discuss one of the following questions with your partner. List the key information, and share your opinion with the class.

(1) If you could create a superhero whose main power is to bring justice, what would their name and superpower be?

(2) If you were the ruler of a kingdom, what unusual punishment would you invent for small misdemeanors?

(3) What would a world where everything is perfectly fair look like?

(4) If you could choose any historical figure to be a judge on a talent show, who would it be and why?

(5) Social media has become an important channel for people to make their voices heard. Is it a step forward or a step backward for social justice?

(6) What innovative ways can college students use to enhance and spread awareness of justice in society?

Section 2 Listening Comprehension

Passage One

Directions: Listen to the following passage. Fill in the blanks with what you hear.

As socialism with Chinese characteristics has entered a new era, the (1) _____ challenge facing Chinese society has evolved. What we now face is the gap between unbalanced and inadequate development and the people's (2) _____ needs for a better life. China has seen the basic needs of over a billion people met, has basically made it possible for people to live (3) _____ lives, and will soon bring the building of a moderately prosperous society to a successful completion. The needs to be met for the people to live better lives are increasingly broad. Not only have their material and cultural needs grown; their demands for democracy, rule of law, (4) _____ and justice, security, and a better environment are increasing. At the same time, China's overall productive forces have significantly improved and in many areas our production capacity (5) _____ the world. The more prominent problem is that our development is unbalanced and inadequate. This has become the main constraining factor in meeting the people's increasing needs for a better life.

The well-being of the people is the (6) _____ goal of development. We must do more to improve the lives and address the concerns of the people and use development to strengthen areas of weakness and promote social fairness and justice. We should make steady progress in ensuring people's (7) _____ to childcare, education, employment, medical services, elderly care, housing, and social assistance.

We will intensify poverty alleviation, see that all our people have a greater sense of (8) _____ as they contribute to and gain from development, and continue to promote well-rounded human development and common (9) _____ for everyone. We will continue the Peaceful China initiative, strengthen and develop new forms of social governance, and ensure social harmony and stability. We must work hard to see that our country enjoys (10) _____ peace and stability and our people live and work in contentment.

Passage Two

Directions: *Listen to the following passage. Fill in the blanks with what you hear.*

China has been actively exploring new channels, domains and models for further (1) _____ Internet technology with judicial activities, according to a White Paper published Thursday. The White Paper titled "China's Law-Based Cyberspace Governance in the New Era" was (2) _____ by China's State Council Information Office. China has been pushing for the (3) _____ of latest technologies such as big data, cloud computing, artificial intelligence and blockchain in judicial (4) _____, judgment enforcement, judicial administration, and other fields, read the document.

It added that local courts are encouraged to explore new (5) _____ with regional features for Internet-empowered adjudication, on the basis of the development of local internet industry and the characteristics of local cyber disputes.

China has (6) _____ legal oversight with big data. It has systematically integrated a wide range of (7) _____ information, worked on models and platforms for big data-based legal oversight, and implemented oversight of the prosecution of individual cases and of similar cases in order to address the common problems they raise, thus improving the quality and efficiency of legal oversight, said the White Paper. "These new models of cyber justice (8) _____ the further development of the socialist judicial system with Chinese characteristics in cyberspace," said the document. It added that Internet (9) _____ represent a success in creating new judicial models, citing the internet courts established in Hangzhou, Beijing and Guangzhou. These courts focus on 11 types of Internet-related disputes in the cities under their jurisdiction, including those (10) _____ online loan contracts, online infringement, and online copyright, said the White Paper.

 Strategies for Better Listening

Listening Skill: Getting Meaning from Context—Knowledge of the Culture, Speaker, or Situation.

According to Encyclopedia Britannica, culture includes knowledge, language, ideas, beliefs, customs, codes, institutions, tools, techniques, works of art, rituals, and ceremonies, among other elements. In the above exercise, if the listener has knowledge in socialism with Chinese characteristics, he or she can easily fill in the following blanks:

"... the contradiction between unbalanced and inadequate development and the people's <u>ever-growing</u> needs for a better life."

"The well-being of the people is the <u>fundamental</u> goal of development."

"It added that Internet <u>courts</u> represent a success in creating new judicial models, citing the internet courts established in Hangzhou, Beijing and Guangzhou."

Exercise

Directions: *Listening to the following dialogue and monologue. Answer the questions.*

(1) Dialogue

A: Could you pass me the salt, please?

B: Sure, here you go.

A: Thanks. You know, in many Asian cultures, it's impolite to pass something with one hand. Using both hands shows more respect.

According to the dialogue, how should people pass salt to others in a respectful way?

a. Using one hand.

b. Using two hands.

c. Using one hand has no difference from two.

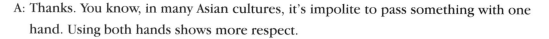

(2) Monologue

What does the word "savvy-shopper" mean?

_____

_____

PART **II** Reading

Section 1　Pre-reading Activity

1. Directions: *The passage you are going to read talks about "environmental justice". In groups, discuss the following questions.*

(1) What does the term "environmental justice" mean to you?

(2) Can you think of any real-life examples where environmental justice issues have arisen?

(3) Why do you think it's important to address environmental justice concerns in society?

2. Directions: *The following are a few lines from the passage. In your opinion, what are they talking about?*

(1) "... climate-related disasters push 26 million people into poverty annually."

(2) "As a result, farmers can grow crops more sustainably..."

(3) "With highly accurate weather forecasting... smallholder farmers can build greater climate resilience..."

(4) "... apps alone are not an antidote to climate injustice."

Advancing Environmental Justice with AI[①]

　　Climate change is undoubtedly the defining challenge of our time, but its effects are not equally distributed. In both developed and developing countries, environmental **degradation** disproportionately affects communities **marginalized** because of race, ethnicity, religion, and poverty. More often than not, these communities are already

_____

① From CGTN.

confronting systemic inequalities such as water scarcity and greater exposure to pollution and extreme weather events—all of which are **exacerbated** by the climate crisis. It is a reality with which I am intimately familiar. As a child, my family had a farm on **Dominica**, a small **Caribbean** island state that faces the threat of hurricanes each year. One tropical storm could knock out power **grids** and wipe out entire harvests, destroying local **livelihoods**.

According to the World Bank, climate-related disasters push 26 million people into poverty annually. And because the world's poorest people often depend on agriculture—a sector highly dependent on favorable weather conditions—to support themselves, they urgently need access to technical, financial, and institutional resources to prepare for and respond to ever more frequent and intense extreme weather events. **Given** its capacity to innovate climate solutions, the technology sector could provide the tools we need to understand, **mitigate**, and even **reverse** the damaging effects of global warming. In fact, addressing **longstanding** environmental injustices requires these companies to put the newest and most effective technologies into the hands of those on the front lines of the climate crisis.

Tools that **harness** the power of artificial intelligence, in particular, could offer **unprecedented** access to accurate information and prediction, enabling communities to learn from and adapt to climate challenges in real time. The IBM Sustainability Accelerator, which was launched in 2022, is at the **forefront** of this effort, supporting the development and scaling of projects such as the Deltares Aquality App, an AI-powered tool that helps farmers assess and improve water quality. As a result, farmers can grow crops more sustainably, prevent **runoff** pollution, and protect **biodiversity**.

Consider also the challenges that **smallholder** farmers face, such as rising costs, the difficulty of competing with larger producers that have better tools and technology, and, of course, the devastating effects of climate change on biodiversity and weather patterns. Accurate information, especially about soil conditions and water availability, can help them address these issues, but these have historically been hard to obtain.

One could imagine regional officials in a developing country **deploying** a machine learning **algorithm** to forecast future population growth and corresponding change in energy demand using temporal and spatial data. With this forecasting model, **policymakers** could **optimize** the country's energy network, redirecting supply to where it will be needed most. That is also something that we are supporting today.

Developing AI-powered mobile apps and virtual assistants, and making them widely available, promote **equitable** access to data and technical insights. With highly accurate weather forecasting, advanced **agronomy** techniques, and carbon-footprint calculations, as well as other predictions generated by AI, smallholder farmers can build greater climate **resilience** and boost both production and income by adapting to changing conditions more quickly and managing crops more sustainably.

At the same time, simply handing over these tools to disadvantaged communities will not solve the problem—apps alone are not an **antidote** to climate injustice. To deploy AI-based technology successfully, tech companies must be willing to share knowledge with users, including instructions on how to take measurements that will yield data. They must build in the ability for users to collaborate independently with one another, and **solicit** feedback from farmers and other users. To that end, an AI chatbot that automates question-and-answer exchanges could help minimize user-training challenges while **democratizing** access to information. As companies develop AI solutions, we also need to support local tech firms and app developers, as they are best positioned to put these tools to use.

Beyond increasing access to new AI-powered tools, the tech community, together with NGOs, governments, and international agencies, can help build an equitable, resilient future for **disenfranchised** communities by providing training in the technical skills and knowledge required for green jobs. As the transition to a low-carbon global economy accelerates, demand for so-called "green skills" is projected to **outstrip** supply. Preparing workers for the jobs of the future, in combination with the widespread adoption of new technologies, will strengthen climate resilience, especially in developing economies.

All of us—individuals, corporations, organizations, and governments—share the responsibility to address growing environmental threats. Tech firms, in particular, must channel more resources to combat global warming. That means investing in the development and deployment of AI tools and ensuring that those in the greatest need can access them. Finding climate solutions—and achieving environmental justice—depends on the private sector **mobilizing** its expertise for the greater good.

(781 words)

 New Words

degradation	/ˌdegrəˈdeɪʃən/	n.	恶化；衰退
marginalize	/ˈmɑːdʒɪnəˌlaɪz/	v.	使边缘化；排挤
exacerbate	/ɪgˈzæsəˌbeɪt/	v.	使……恶化
Dominica	/ˌdɒmɪˈniːkə/	n.	多米尼加

Caribbean	/kəˈrɪbiːən/	n.	加勒比海；加勒比海人
		adj.	加勒比海的
grid	/grɪd/	n.	网格
livelihood	/ˈlaɪvlɪˌhʊd/	n.	生计
given	/ˈgɪvən/	prep.	考虑到
mitigate	/ˈmɪtɪˌgeɪt/	v.	缓解
reverse	/rɪˈvɜːs/	v.	转向；颠倒
longstanding	/ˌlɒŋˈstændɪŋ/	adj.	长期存在的
harness	/ˈhɑːnɪs/	v.	利用
		n.	马具；挽具
unprecedented	/ʌnˈpresɪˌdentɪd/	adj.	史无前例的
forefront	/ˈfɔːˌfrʌnt/	n.	前沿；重心
runoff	/ˈrʌnɔːf/	n.	径流；流走的东西
biodiversity	/ˌbaɪəʊdaɪˈvɜːsɪtɪ/	n.	生物多样性
smallholder	/ˈsmɔːlhəʊldə(r)/	n.	小农；小佃农
deploy	/dɪˈplɔɪ/	v.	部署
algorithm	/ˈælgəˌrɪðəm/	n.	（计算机）演算法
policymaker	/ˈpɒlɪsɪˌmeɪkə/	n.	政策制定者；决策人
optimize	/ˈɒptɪˌmaɪz/	v.	使优化
equitable	/ˈekwɪtəb(ə)l/	adj.	公平合理的
agronomy	/əˈgrɒnəmɪ/	n.	农艺学
resilience	/rɪˈzɪlɪəns/	n.	恢复力，复原力
antidote	/ˈæntɪˌdəʊt/	n.	解毒药
solicit	/səˈlɪsɪt/	v.	请求给予
democratize	/dɪˈmɒkrəˌtaɪz/	v.	使民主化
disenfranchise	/ˌdɪsɪnˈfræntʃaɪz/	v.	剥夺（某人群的）权力
outstrip	/ˌaʊtˈstrɪp/	v.	超过
mobilize	/ˈməʊbɪˌlaɪz/	v.	动员

 ## Phrases and Expressions

| more often than not | 通常；大体上 |
| knock out | 破坏 |

wipe out	摧毁；使灭绝
hand over	交给……负责
to that end	为此
in combinatbon with	与……结合

Section 2   Reading Comprehension

1. Directions: *Read the passage as quickly as you can. Answer the questions.*

(1) Where did the author's family have a farm when he was a child?

(2) What threat does Dominica face annually?

(3) What sector is mentioned as highly dependent on favorable weather conditions?

(4) How does the text suggest the technology sector can contribute to addressing climate change?

(5) What example is provided regarding the use of machine learning in a developing country?

2. Directions: *Read the passage again. Decide whether the following statements are true (T) or false (F).*

(1) Environmental degradation disproportionately affects marginalized communities globally.   (   )

(2) Smallholder farmers face challenges including rising costs and difficulty of competing with larger producers.   (   )

(3) The IBM Sustainability Accelerator was launched in 2023.   (   )

(4) The Deltares Aquality App aims to assess and improve air quality.   (   )

(5) Deploying AI technology successfully requires collaboration and knowledge sharing.
                                                                    (   )

(6) AI chatbots are mentioned as a replacement for user training challenges.   (   )

(7) The tech community can contribute to building a resilient future by providing training for green jobs.   (   )

(8) The demand for green skills is projected to decline in the transition to a low-carbon global economy.   (   )

What Do You Think?

3. Directions: Discuss the followings in small groups or pairs. Then report to the class.

(1) The passage emphasizes how climate change disproportionately affects marginalized communities. Can you provide examples from both developed and developing countries that illustrate how these communities are particularly vulnerable to the impacts of environmental degradation and extreme weather events?

(2) The passage discusses the potential of AI-powered tools in addressing climate challenges. Can you discuss some specific examples of how AI can be applied to assist communities in adapting to climate change, beyond the mentioned Deltares Aquality App?

(3) The passage mentions that simply providing AI tools is not enough to address climate injustice. What challenges do you foresee in deploying AI-based technology effectively in marginalized communities, and how can these challenges be overcome, especially in terms of knowledge sharing and user engagement?

(4) The passage suggests that preparing workers for "green jobs" is essential for climate resilience. Could you elaborate on what green jobs are and provide examples? How can governments, NGOs, and the private sector collaborate to ensure that individuals in marginalized communities have access to training and employment opportunities in these fields?

(5) The passage highlights the importance of tech companies sharing knowledge and building collaborative features in AI tools. How can AI-based technology effectively engage and empower local communities, particularly those with limited access to technology and resources, to actively participate in climate resilience efforts?

(6) The passage suggests that addressing climate change and environmental justice requires cooperation between individuals, corporations, organizations, and governments. What are some examples of successful international collaborations or initiatives aimed at promoting environmental justice and mitigating the impacts of climate change? How can such collaborations be expanded and strengthened?

Vocabulary

4. Directions: Read the following sentences. Search the text for words that mean the same as those underlined.

(1) Climate change has the potential to **worsen** existing water shortages in many

regions, making access to clean water an even greater challenge.

(2) Tourism plays a vital role in **sustaining the economic well-being** of the coastal town, with hotels, restaurants, and local artisans depending on visitors for their income.

(3) The company's commitment to customer satisfaction has consistently positioned it **at the industry's cutting edge**, earning it a strong reputation for quality service.

(4) Athletes and trainers focus on **fine-tuning and perfecting** nutrition and training regimens to achieve peak performance during competitions.

(5) The educational system is increasingly recognizing the importance of instilling students with the skills to **navigate life's challenges with strength and flexibility**.

5. Directions: *Complete the following sentences with the correct form of words from the text.*

(1) G _____ the circumstances, it was a remarkable achievement that she completed the project ahead of schedule.

(2) Planting trees in urban areas can help **m** _____ the effects of air pollution by absorbing harmful pollutants from the atmosphere.

(3) Engineers are working on innovative ways to **h** _____ the energy generated by ocean currents to provide sustainable electricity to coastal communities.

(4) In the world of technology, companies often **d** _____ beta versions of their software to gather user feedback before the official release.

(5) The government's efforts to provide **e** _____ access to quality education have resulted in improved literacy rates among underserved communities.

(6) In case of a snakebite, it's crucial to administer the appropriate **a** _____ as quickly as possible to counteract the venom's effects.

(7) Despite initial doubts, the athletes' determination and hard work allowed them to **o** _____ their own previous records, achieving a remarkable level of performance.

(8) The community quickly **m** _____ volunteers and resources to provide aid after the natural disaster, demonstrating the power of collective action in times of crisis.

6. Directions: *Complete the following sentences by selecting suitable phrases in the box.*

more often than not	knock out	wipe out
hand over	to that end	in combination with

(1) The company implemented new sustainability initiatives, including reducing waste and promoting energy efficiency, _____, they aimed to minimize their environmental impact.

(2) The new smartphone model boasts advanced camera technology _____ enhanced image processing software, resulting in stunning photography capabilities.

(3) While traveling, you'll find that cultural misunderstandings can be easily resolved with patience and open communication, as _____, people appreciate respectful efforts to understand their customs and traditions.

(4) As a gesture of goodwill, the diplomat agreed to _____ the confidential documents to the international peacekeeping organization for further investigation.

PART III Understanding Global Issues

 Strategies for Better Speaking

Speaking Skill: Informative Speech vs. Persuasive Speech

The main purpose of an informative speech is literally to inform, while a persuasive speech to persuade. Depending on the occasion and purpose, a speaker should decide whether it's going to inform only or inform and persuade the audience once he or she has collected all the ideas on the content. Informative speeches, introducing an object, a process, an event, or a concept, focus on When, Who, What, Where, How equally, while persuasive speeches focus more on the Why, explaining with facts, adequate data or stories to the audience the reason for their future action.

Exercise

Directions: *Work with your partner and come up with a 3-minute speech that features the topic of justice, following the seven steps below. Please also refer to the four questions below as your prompts.*

Step 1: Work with your partner and brainstorm the cluster of words related to justice.

Step 2: Read the following four questions and choose the one that interests you the most.

Step 3: Discuss with your partner your own understanding and experiences on the topic.

Step 4: Work out an outline for your main points on the topic.

Step 5: Search for important details or key information to the development of your speech.

Step 6: Sort out all the supporting points collected and develop your arguments in a certain order.

Step 7: Take turns to present the body part of the speech to each other and polish the supporting sentences till both of you are satisfied.

(1) What is the role of forgiveness in the pursuit of justice?

(2) In what ways do technology and the digital age impact our understanding and pursuit of justice?

(3) How does the concept of environmental justice relate to the distribution of environmental benefits and harms among different communities?

(4) What are the responsibilities of individuals in promoting justice in their communities and societies?

Unit 6

Morality

PART **I** Listening and Speaking

Section 1 Pre-listening Activity

Directions: Browse the questions below and discuss one of the following questions with your partner. List the key information, and share your opinion with the class.

(1) Do you have a role model? Who is he or she? What makes him or her a good role model?

(2) Which historical figures are celebrated for their actions that were considered moral?

(3) If you could invent a new holiday that celebrates a moral value, what would it be called and how would people celebrate it?

(4) If you discovered a new planet and had the chance to create its moral code from scratch, what key values would you include?

(5) If you could implement one universal moral principle that everyone in the world had to follow, what would it be and why?

(6) What ethical obligations should students uphold to ensure academic integrity?

Section 2 Listening Comprehension

Passage One

Directions: Listen to the passage. Decide whether the statements are true (T) or false (F).

(1) This passage is mainly about how to make moral judgements. ( )

(2) Responses to moral dilemmas often depend on some factors, such as decision-makers' relationship to the involved parties, how the action would be carried out, and whether these decisions are made in a foreign or native language. ( )

(3) In the footbridge dilemma, people are willing to sacrifice one person in order to save five, especially when they are using their native language. ( )

(4) The results of the moral dilemma were not consistent when people are from different language backgrounds. ( )

(5) According to a recent study, when people use a foreign language, they think more before making moral decisions. ( )

Passage Two

Directions: Listen to the passage. Fill in the blanks with what you hear.

The theme of science fiction seems closer to reality with the (1) _____ of ChatGPT, an artificial intelligence (AI) language model developed by OpenAI. With its remarkable ability to (2) _____ human-like responses to a wide range of questions, ChatGPT has left the world in awe of the potential of AI. However, at the same time, there is a crucial need to analyze the (3) _____ impacts of AI, because without strict regulations, one could see the following challenges in the near future. Plagiarism: A recent survey showed that 89 percent of students (4) _____ to using OpenAI's platform for assistance to complete their assignments.

The problem is that the written output created by AI can lead to a rise in plagiarism and concerns about academic (5) _____. Misrepresentation: The use of AI language models such as ChatGPT may generate fake identities because chatbots can produce texts that (6) _____ those written by a real person.

(7) _____ violations: The digital agent can gather huge amounts of personal information, including addresses, dates of birth, phone numbers and financial information that can be used for various types of cybercrime. Undetermined responsibility: These AI systems are often operated by (8) _____ parties including the developer, platform provider and even the user. Although their purpose is to provide accurate information, mistakes can still occur. In such cases, it can be difficult to determine who should be held responsible for these errors and who should be held accountable for the consequences.

Bias and (9) _____: A study in 2018 found that the widely used language model, GPT-2, was biased in favour of gender stereotypes. For example, it was more likely to associate male pronouns with professionals like engineers and doctors. The rise of AI language models such as ChatGPT has brought us closer to a world once imagined only in science fictions. The potential of these technologies is immense and (10) _____, but it is important to consider the risks associated with their use.

Strategies for Better Listening

Listening Skill: Identifying Logical Connectives

Logical connectives play a crucial role across various aspects of English language skills, including listening, speaking, reading, and writing. Mastering these connectives in listening exercises enables listeners to accurately comprehend the speaker's underlying thoughts and intentions. They serve as guideposts, indicating the development of ideas or thoughts in the discourse. Common logical connectives often function as transitional words, serving different purposes:

Enumerating: first of all, in the first place, to begin with, after that

Exemplifying: for example, for instance, in particular, particularly, such as, that is to say, as a matter of fact, namely, take... as an example, such as, that is, like, as follows, in other words

Restating: in other words, rather, to put it simply

Selected: alternatively, on the other hand, then again

Progressive: what's more, furthermore, on one hand... on the other hand..., in addition to, moreover, worse still, to make matters worse, but for, besides

Contrasting: conversely, in comparison, in contrast to, instead, on the contrary

Conceding: after all, all the same, though, although, even though, even if, in spite of, despite this, despite that, nevertheless, nonetheless, still, except for, in fact

Equivalence: in the same way, likewise, similarly

Summarizing: in conclusion, in summary, to conclude, to sum up, in short, briefly, in brief, generally speaking, in a word, as you know, as is known to all

Result: as a result, consequently, hence, so, therefore, thanks to, thus, therefore, as a result of, with the help of, owe... to...

Inferring: in other words, in that case, then, (or) else, otherwise

Initiating: to begin with, according to, so far, as far as

Temporal: first, firstly, in the meantime, at the same time, for the first time, ever since, while, shortly after, the next moment, nowadays, at present, before long, in the future

Spatial: on the right/left, to the right/left, on one side of, on the other side of, in the middle/center of

There are many logical connectives in the above, such as the following sentence:

The only way to save them would be to push a fat bystander onto the tracks, thereby killing him but stopping the train. The connective words "thereby" and "but" hereby serve as logical transitions telling the listener "killing him (the fat bystander)" would be the result and "stopping the train (to save the five people)" is a different situation rather than being killed by the oncoming electric vehicle.

PART **II** Reading

Section 1 Pre-reading Activity

1. Directions: *The passage you are going to read talks about "Chinese philosophy". In groups, discuss the following questions.*

(1) Can you name any Chinese philosophers or key principles in Chinese philosophy?

(2) What potential connections have you seen between Chinese philosophy and daily life in China?

(3) How might Chinese philosophy contribute to a global understanding of different worldviews?

2. Directions: *The following are a few lines from the passage. In your opinion, what are they talking about?*

(1) "... there is a powerful trend toward viewing the world only in instrumental or material terms..."

(2) "Both Western and Chinese philosophical traditions emphasize the importance of openness and dialogue..."

(3) "... the mainstream Chinese philosophies of Confucianism, Taoism, and Buddhism can all present a quite different image of China..."

(4) "... it is important to understand the various trends in Western engagement with Chinese thought in modern history..."

Mainstream Chinese Philosophies Present a Different Image of China to the World①

Interviewer (I): You have studied Chinese ancient philosophy for many years. What do you think of **Confucianism's** value in today's society?

Benjamin (B): In contemporary society, whether at the level of people or countries, there is a powerful trend toward viewing the world only in instrumental or material terms, such as the concept of "human resources" in which people are **equated** to material or financial resources to be utilized for maximum gain, not in terms of human

---

① From *China Daily*.

relationships such as families, colleagues, and friends, which leads to **dehumanization**, loss of **ethical** values, **alienation**, etc.

While this is often associated with Western **modernity** and capitalism, as analyzed by philosophers such as Karl Marx and Herbert Marcuse, a quite similar situation occurred in Ancient China with the decline of the Zhou Dynasty and the "collapse of **ritual** and music" in the Spring and Autumn (770 BC—476 BC) and Warring States (475 BC—221 BC) periods, in which many of the Chinese ruling classes (kings, ministers, etc.) began to view the world simply in terms of "benefit" for themselves and their states, and similar crises recurred throughout Chinese history, e.g. at the end of the Han Dynasty (206 BC—220 AD). Much of the classic Confucian thought of Confucius, Mencius, Zhu Xi, Wang Yangming, etc. was an attempt to respond to such a crisis by promoting humanistic values such as **benevolence**, **righteousness**, **propriety**, wisdom, and **trustworthiness**, restoring a focus on the moral and ethical aspects of human nature, such as Mencius' focus on cultivating our inherent moral instincts and Wang Yangming's "extension of innate moral knowing". Since many problems in modern society are **comparable** to this situation, Confucianism can have an important role to play in addressing these issues.

I: What are the similarities between Western and Chinese philosophy?

B: Superficially, there are many differences between the two, such as Western philosophy's focus on logical argument and abstract problems **detached** from human life as opposed to Chinese philosophy's focus on holistic understanding and social questions.

However, I think if we look at how the two traditions emerged, we can see a fundamental common approach shared between them. Both developed at a similar period in human history (Jaspers' so-called "**Axial** Age") when Zhou Dynasty China and Ancient Greece saw a decline of traditional state-religious forms of society, and when economic growth and technological advances led to a social crisis: How can a rapidly changing society achieve lasting order, harmony, and stability? As Jean-Pierre Vernant argued, like early Chinese thought, Greek philosophy developed its **cosmologies** and **ontologies** against this background, seeking a "new image of the world" through a human-centered approach in which people take the initiative in collectively structuring human existence and understanding and resolving social problems. Both Western and Chinese philosophical traditions emphasize the importance of openness and dialogue, and strive to attain a "cosmic" plane that transcends individual interests and prejudices, "seeing things from the perspective of the Dao" in Zhuangzi, and grasping the common "**logos**" of the world in Greek thought. They also both connect this to building a human community of equal "friends" where such openness and dialogue can take place, where **civilized** human beings can work towards achieving basic **consensus** in our common social life.

I: In your opinion, how would spreading Chinese philosophy contribute to building a community with a shared future?

B: One of the biggest problems we face today is the apparent lack of serious dialogue on values at the global level. In this regard, China's **portrayal** in much Western media often fits into the latter narrative, focusing on increased material wealth and **pragmatic realpolitik**, etc. While these aspects are present in some traditional Chinese philosophy, particularly from the Warring States period (e.g. Sunzi's Art of War, the **Legalism** of Shang Yang and Han Feizi, etc.), the **mainstream** Chinese philosophies of Confucianism, **Taoism** and Buddhism can all present a quite different image of China, one that implies strong ethical and political positions on various contemporary issues, can engage with the global community on issues facing **humanity** as a whole (climate change, poverty, war, pollution, etc.), and contribute a Chinese perspective to forming a global consensus on basic norms and rules.

I: Could you give some advice on promoting Chinese philosophy internationally?

B: Although there has been some progress in this regard, we still need to work on overcoming **outdated** prejudices concerning "Chinese philosophy" in the West, especially the view that it is more of a "**spiritual** tradition" than "serious philosophy".

All too often the view of Chinese philosophy as an organic part of "Chinese traditional culture" doesn't help in this respect, since it can give the impression that Chinese philosophy is a museum-piece that is only of historical interest, rather than a diverse group of approaches that can provide important perspectives on contemporary philosophical problems.

In promoting Chinese philosophy, it is important to understand the various trends in Western engagement with Chinese thought in modern history, e.g. Leibniz and early understandings of Confucianism, spiritual approaches to Taoism and Buddhism in Western **mysticism**, Martin Heidegger's engagement with Taoism, **synthetic** approaches to Confucianism and American pragmatism, and recent interest in virtue ethics. This can show that Chinese philosophy is an "open tradition" that can be connected with other philosophical traditions through many different paths.

(878 words)

New Words

Confucianism	/kənˈfjuːʃəˌnɪzəm/	n.	儒家；儒学
equate	/ɪˈkweɪt/	v.	将……等同于；等同于
dehumanization	/diːˌhjuːmənaɪˈzeɪʃn/	v.	去人性化
ethical	/ˈeθɪkəl/	adj.	道德上的
alienation	/ˌeɪljəˈneɪʃən/	n.	疏远
modernity	/mɒˈdɜːnɪtɪ/	n.	现代性
ritual	/ˈrɪtjʊəl/	n.	宗教仪式；典礼
		adj.	仪式性的；传统的
benevolence	/bəˈnevələns/	n.	仁慈；仁爱
righteousness	/ˈraɪtʃəsnəs/	n.	正义；正直
propriety	/prəˈpraɪətɪ/	n.	礼仪；得体
trustworthiness	/ˈtrʌstwɜːðɪnəs/	n.	诚信；可信赖
comparable	/ˈkɒmpərəbəl/	adj.	相当的；可比的
detach	/dɪˈtætʃ/	v.	脱离；分开
axial	/ˈæksɪəl/	adj.	轴的；成轴的
cosmology	/kɒzˈmɒlədʒɪ/	n.	宇宙学
ontology	/ɒnˈtɒlədʒɪ/	n.	本体论
logos	/ˈlɒɡɒs/	n.	理性
civilized	/ˈsɪvɪˌlaɪzd/	adj.	文明的；有教养的
consensus	/kənˈsensəs/	n.	共识
portrayal	/pɔːˈtreɪəl/	n.	扮演；描绘；刻画
pragmatic	/præɡˈmætɪk/	adj.	务实的
realpolitik	/reɪˈɑːlpɒlɪˈtiːk/	n.	实力政治
legalism	/ˈliːɡəˌlɪzəm/	n.	法家；恪守法律条规
Taoism	/ˈtaʊɪzəm/	n.	道教
mainstream	/ˈmeɪnˌstriːm/	n.	主流
humanity	/hjuːˈmænɪtɪ/	n.	人类；人性；人文学科
outdated	/ˌaʊtˈdeɪtɪd/	adj.	过时的
spiritual	/ˈspɪrɪtjʊəl/	adj.	精神的；宗教的
mysticism	/ˈmɪstɪˌsɪzəm/	n.	神秘主义
synthetic	/sɪnˈθetɪk/	adj.	合成的

Phrases and Expressions

as opposed to	与……相对
take the initiative	采取主动
in this regard	在这方面
fit into	适应；符合
engage with	与……互动
rather than	而不是

Section 2   Reading Comprehension

1. Directions: *Read the passage as quickly as you can. Answer the questions.*

(1) In which historical periods in Ancient China did the decline of the Zhou Dynasty and the "collapse of ritual and music" occur?

(2) Who are some of the classic Confucian thinkers mentioned by Benjamin in the text?

(3) According to Benjamin, what values did Confucian thought attempt to promote in response to the crisis in Ancient China?

(4) According to Benjamin, what is one of the biggest problems faced today in terms of global values dialogue?

(5) In promoting Chinese philosophy internationally, what aspect does Benjamin suggest needs to be overcome in the West?

2. Directions: *Read the passage again. Decide whether the following statements are true (T) or false (F).*

(1) Benjamin associates the concept of "human resources" primarily with Western modernity and capitalism. ( )

(2) The passage suggests that Confucianism might not be relevant to addressing modern societal issues that mirror historical crises in Ancient China. ( )

(3) Benjamin argues that both Western and Chinese philosophical traditions emerged during a period known as the "Axial Age". ( )

(4) According to Benjamin, Western philosophy's primary focus revolves around logical argument and abstract problems. ( )

(5) The passage mentions that the mainstream Chinese philosophies emphasize strong ethics. ( )

(6) In the West, there is a view that "Chinese philosophy" is more of a "spiritual tradition" than "serious philosophy".　　　　　　　　　　　(　)

(7) The view of Chinese philosophy as an organic part of "Chinese traditional culture" helps overcome the outdated prejudices regarding "Chinese philosophy".　(　)

(8) Chinese philosophy is a flexible tradition, able to intertwine with diverse philosophical approaches.　　　　　　　　　　　　　　　　(　)

What Do You Think?

3. Directions: *Discuss the following in small groups or pairs. Then report to the class.*

(1) Benjamin draws parallels between the decline of the Zhou Dynasty and crises in Ancient China with contemporary challenges. How do you interpret the recurrence of similar crises in Chinese history, and do you agree that Confucianism's emphasis on humanistic values provides a viable response to such situations?

(2) Benjamin mentions the crisis response in both Western and Chinese philosophies during pivotal historical periods. Can you compare and contrast how Confucianism addressed crises in Ancient China with the responses of Western philosophy during the Axial Age? Are there distinct approaches or shared principles in their crisis management strategies?

(3) According to Benjamin, Confucius thought aims to restore a focus on moral and ethical aspects. How do you see Confucianism addressing the cultivation of moral instincts, as highlighted by Mencius? In what ways can these concepts contribute to ethical restoration in the present?

(4) Benjamin emphasizes the importance of openness and dialogue in both Western and Chinese philosophies. How can these shared principles contribute to cross-cultural understanding and collaboration in our contemporary globalized society? Are there specific challenges or opportunities that arise when integrating these philosophical principles into modern intercultural dialogues?

(5) Benjamin highlights the challenge of outdated prejudices regarding "Chinese philosophy" in the West. What specific stereotypes or misconceptions do you think hinder a more nuanced understanding of Chinese philosophical traditions? How can these stereotypes be addressed to foster a more open and receptive global reception of Chinese philosophy?

(6) Given the diverse paths through which Chinese philosophy can connect with other

traditions, how might this integration influence not only academic philosophy but also practical aspects of international relations, policy-making, and cultural exchange? What potential benefits and challenges do you foresee in the real-world application of a more globally inclusive philosophical dialogue?

Vocabulary

4. Directions: *Read the following sentences. Search the passage for words that mean the same as those underlined.*

(1) In the workplace, a lack of communication and recognition can contribute to feelings of **isolation and estrangement** among employees.

(2) The **kindness** of the volunteers at the animal shelter shines through as they dedicate their time and care to the well-being of the rescued animals.

(3) Despite the challenges, the diplomatic negotiations remained **polite and cultured**, with representatives maintaining a respectful and constructive dialogue throughout the process.

(4) In the spirit of collaboration, the team worked together to establish a **common agreement** on the project timeline, ensuring that everyone's input was considered and valued.

(5) The new technology quickly gained popularity and became **widely accepted** as more people adopted it for daily use.

5. Directions: *Complete the following sentences with the correct form of words from the passage.*

(1) It's essential to dress with **p** _____ when attending formal events, adhering to the expected standards of clothing.

(2) The artist's **p** _____ of the scenic landscape captured the beauty and peacefulness of the natural surroundings.

(3) It is a common mistake to **e** _____ wealth with happiness, as true contentment often stems from personal relationships and fulfillment.

(4) The architecture of the new building reflects the principles of **m** _____, featuring sleek lines and innovative design elements.

(5) Her achievements in the field are truly remarkable and, in terms of impact, are **c** _____ to those of pioneers who came before her.

(6) Teaching students about **e** _____ decision-making is an essential component of their education, preparing them to navigate complex moral dilemmas in their future careers.

(7) The advancement of technology should always be guided by considerations for the well-being of **h** _____, ensuring it serves to enhance rather than detract from our collective progress.

(8) In business, a **p** _____ approach involves making decisions based on available resources and market conditions rather than relying on idealistic goals.

6. Directions: *Complete the following sentences by selecting suitable phrases in the box.*

as opposed to	take the initiative	in this regard
fit into	engage with	rather than

(1) The restaurant offers a variety of vegetarian dishes _____ just focusing on meat-based options to cater to a diverse clientele.

(2) To excel in a competitive job market, it's essential for individuals to _____ in acquiring new skills and staying updated with industry trends.

(3) Mary prefers to work independently, _____ being part of a large team, to maximize her productivity and creativity.

(4) Teachers strive to create interactive lessons that encourage students to _____ the material, fostering a deeper understanding of the subject.

PART III Understanding Global Issues

Strategies for Better Speaking

Speaking Skill: Comparisons and Contrasts

It is a very global skill that when you compare two or more things, you need to talk about similarities and differences between them. It is also true when you compare two processes or views. The structure of a compare-and-contrast part in speeches is to know when to talk about which subject. Basically, there are three options: subject by subject, meaning you discuss one subject in full and then move on to the next subject; point by point, meaning you discuss one subject's take on a certain aspect and then another subject's take immediately afterward, followed by a new aspect; and similarities and differences, meaning you discuss all the similarities (differences) between your subjects and then all the differences (similarities).

Exercise

Directions: *Work with your partner and come up with a 3-minute story that features the topic of ethics, following the seven steps below. Please also refer to the four questions below as your prompts.*

Step 1: Think up one story that comes to your mind immediately after you see this topic of ethics.

Step 2: Review the details of story or the social issue with help of Internet search.

Step 3: Tell your partner the story and how you felt at the beginning of the incident and how you feel towards it now.

Step 4: Together, analyze the reason(s) of the difference(s) in your understanding of the same incident.

Step 5: Read the following questions and choose the one closest to your story.

Step 6: Retell the story you shared with the help from the question.

Step 7: Explain how the story might have changed if the major ethical concern had been different in the beginning.

(1) What is the role of ethics in our everyday lives, and why is it important?

(2) How do ethical considerations come into play in various professions, such as medicine, business, and journalism?

(3) How does technology, such as AI and genetic engineering, raise ethical concerns, and what guidelines should be in place to address them?

(4) How do the media and entertainment industry impact our ethical values and perceptions?

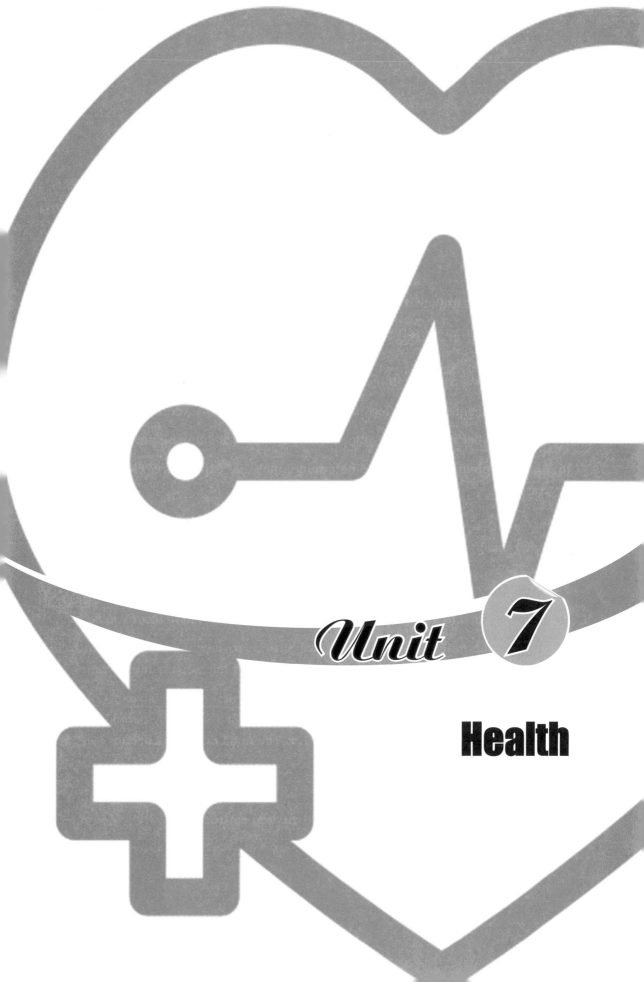

Unit 7

Health

PART **I** Listening and Speaking

Section 1 Pre-listening Activity

Directions: Browse the questions below and discuss one of the following questions with your partner. List the key information, and share your opinion with the class.

(1) What are the two cities with the highest life expectancy in the world? What factors do you believe contribute to their longevity?

(2) Who is the oldest person you have ever known or met? Please tell his or her secrets to a long life.

(3) What are some common unhealthy habits that modern people often have?

(4) How does mental health affect physical well-being, and vice versa?

(5) How does diet and nutrition influence overall health and disease prevention?

(6) In your opinion, does income determine one's life expectancy? Please state your reasons.

Section 2 Listening Comprehension

Passage One

Directions: Listen to the following passage. Fill in the blanks with what you hear.

Health authorities in Taiyuan, capital of Shanxi Province, have listed seven factors that contribute to (1) _____, according to a report released on Tuesday.

The report, issued by the Taiyuan Health Commission and Taiyuan Committee on Aging, was based on a six-month (2) _____ of 166 elderly people who are a hundred years old or older in Taiyuan in 2021. The number of centenarians (百岁老人) in the city reached 178 in 2022.

The seven factors are:

• Favorable geographic, residential, and medical environments

• (3) _____ factors

• A warm and harmonious family (4) _____

- (5) _____ conditions

- A healthy lifestyle

- A calm and optimistic (6) _____

- Adequate elderly care provided by medical and nursing institutions

The report also suggested promoting the concept of active aging and healthy aging, developing a comprehensive and (7) _____ supportive elderly care system, and fostering a society that respects and supports the elderly.

On the personal level, the report also emphasized the cultivation of a positive mindset, adopting good lifestyle habits, and prioritizing (8) _____ and family support.

The health conditions of centenarians not only reflect the quality and level of elderly services provided in the city, but also demonstrate the robustness of the population's (9) _____ well-being and the prosperity of society.

According to data from the Ministry of Civil Affairs, as of the end of 2012, there were 56,000 centenarians nationwide. In August, Li Changguan, Vice-Chairman of the Guangxi Zhuang Autonomous Region, said that there are nearly 7,000 people aged 100 and above in Guangxi, (10) _____ for approximately one-tenth of the national total.

Passage Two

Directions: *Listen to the following passage. Fill in the blanks with what you hear.*

Founded in 1948, World Health Organization (WHO) is the United Nations (1) _____ that connects nations, partners and people to promote health, keep the world safe and serve the (2) _____ — so everyone, everywhere can attain the highest level of health. WHO leads global efforts to (3) _____ universal health coverage. We direct and coordinate the world's response to health (4) _____. And we promote healthier lives—from pregnancy care through old age. Our Triple Billion targets outline an ambitious plan for the world to achieve good health for all using (5) _____-based policies and programmes.

Working with 194 member states across six regions and on the ground in 150+ locations, the WHO team works to improve everyone's ability to enjoy good health and (6) _____. Collaboration is greatly valued by WHO. From governments and (7) _____ society to international organizations, foundations, advocates, researchers and health workers, WHO (8) _____ every part of society to advance the health and security of all. WHO's work remains firmly rooted in the basic principles of the right to health and well-being for all people, as outlined in our 1948 Constitution. The World Health Assembly is the decision-making body of WHO and is attended by (9) _____ from all member states. WHO is committed to the principle of accountability—a core value for an organization that is (10) _____ by countries and other donors to use limited resources effectively to protect and improve global health.

Strategies for Better Listening

Listening Skill: Shorthand in Spot Dictation

The challenge in filling the blanks in a spot dictation relies in putting down the word within in a very limited time, as the content in each line is crucial for the understanding of the whole passage. Therefore, writing the abbreviation of the word missing instead of the complete form is an effective way to save time while listening. The rules of abbreviating long words include:

- Keeping the letters in the beginning syllable and missing the later part, especially the ending vowel(s), *e.g. Medical—Med. Brazil—Bra*

- Compacting the letters while keeping the consonant selectively, *e.g. Japanese—Jpn*

- Country names are abbreviated by keeping the beginning part if they are single words and initials if longer expressions, *e.g. Democratic People's Republic of Korea—D.P.R.K.*

Exercises

1. Directions: *Guess and write the complete form of the following abbreviations you might see in a supermarket.*

(1) RSTD CHKN SDWC

_____

(2) SHVG & HRCT

_____

(3) BODY LOTN

_____

(4) WSNG PWDR

---

2. Directions: *Choose five words from the above listening passages. Write their abbreviated forms.*

1. _____ — _____

2. _____ — _____

3. _____ — _____

4. _____ — _____

5. _____ — _____

PART **II** Reading

Section 1   Pre-reading Activity

1. Directions: *The passage you are going to read talks about "healthcare". In groups, discuss the following questions.*

(1) Have you ever encountered a personal healthcare experience, either positive or negative, that left a lasting impression on you?

(2) In your view, what are the ethical considerations involved in providing healthcare globally?

(3) Can you think of any successful examples of international collaboration in addressing healthcare challenges?

2. Directions: *The following are a few lines from the passage. In your opinion, what are they talking about?*

(1) "The CPHC comprises a diverse array of stakeholders, including hospitals, nursing and auxiliary medical institutions..."

(2) "... provides invaluable insights for Pakistan as it strives to strengthen its own healthcare system."

(3) "The CPHC aligns with Sustainable Development Goal 3..."

(4) "The CPHC is not just a physical link but a pathway towards health diplomacy..."

China-Pakistan Health Corridor on Bilateral Healthcare[1]

The China-Pakistan Health **Corridor** (CPHC), an integral component of the CPEC, stands as a **testament** to the power of collaboration and visionary leadership in times of health crises. In the wake of the coronavirus outbreak, I, as an **eyewitness**, experienced the remarkable courage and cooperation of the Chinese nation in preventing and controlling this deadly virus. The rapid establishment of hospitals and health infrastructure, accomplished within days, highlighted the effectiveness of China's response. In 2006, when I was a student at Shandong University, the idea was **conceived** by me to establish the CPHC to make a significant contribution to the health sector in both China and Pakistan. Fast forward to 2013, this idea saw an opportunity to bring about transformative change in **healthcare**. The result was the establishment of the CPHC, a **multidisciplinary** collaboration aimed at **bolstering** healthcare infrastructure, knowledge exchange and mutual cooperation between the two nations.

The CPHC comprises a diverse **array** of stakeholders, including hospitals, nursing and **auxiliary** medical institutions, research and training centers, IT firms, and **pharmaceutical** industries. This comprehensive approach reflects a commitment to addressing various aspects of healthcare, from service delivery to research and technological innovation. Key initiatives include mobile hospitals, which allow for the extension of medical services to remote and **underserved** areas, addressing one of the critical challenges in Pakistan's healthcare system. This initiative brings healthcare closer to the people, improving **accessibility** and promoting preventive care. Next is technology integration which **leverages** cutting-edge technologies such as artificial intelligence, virtual reality and big data.

The CPHC is at the forefront of healthcare innovation, enhancing **diagnostic** capabilities, **streamlining** data management and facilitating efficient healthcare delivery. The other key initiative is pharmaceutical collaboration, promoting the exchange of knowledge and resources, fostering the development of high-quality and affordable medications. This initiative contributes not only to the **well-being** of the population but also to the economic growth of both nations.

The Chinese experience in managing and controlling health crises, exemplified by their response to COVID-19, provides **invaluable** insights for Pakistan as it strives to strengthen its own healthcare system. The coordinated and **swift** response became a **hallmark** of China's success in preventing and controlling the spread of the coronavirus,

---

① From *China Daily*.

showcasing the nation's resilience and commitment to public health.

The CPHC aligns with Sustainable Development Goal 3, which emphasizes the importance of good health and well-being. By sharing expertise and adopting best practices, this initiative contributes significantly to building a resilient healthcare infrastructure that can **withstand** current and future challenges. The CPHC is not just a one-way transfer of knowledge; it represents mutual cooperation and a win-win situation for both nations. As China shares its advancements in healthcare, Pakistan **reciprocates** with its unique insights and experiences, fostering a collaborative environment that benefits both countries.

The success of China's coordinated response to the coronavirus can be attributed to the collective efforts of its people, backed by a government that prioritized the health and well-being of its citizens. The rapid construction of hospitals, implementation of **stringent** measures, and the mobilization of resources demonstrated the efficiency and effectiveness of China's **pandemic** response strategy. The experience of China in managing health crises can be invaluable for other countries, especially those involved in the Belt and Road Initiative (BRI). The CPHC, an extension of the CPEC, provides a unique opportunity for collaboration in health diplomacy. By leveraging Chinese expertise and resources, BRI countries can enhance their capacity for **epidemic** prevention, control and healthcare infrastructure development.

The CPHC facilitates the exchange of knowledge, technology and resources, paving the way for a collective effort in addressing health challenges within the BRI framework. BRI countries can benefit from China's experience by sharing expertise in epidemic prevention, control measures and healthcare infrastructure development. Collaborative efforts through the CPHC can contribute to the capacity building of healthcare professionals, equipping them with the skills needed to tackle health crises effectively. The collaboration can lead to the development of robust healthcare infrastructure, ensuring that BRI countries are better prepared to handle emergencies and provide quality healthcare to their citizens. Joint efforts in research and development can **accelerate** the discovery of **vaccines**, treatments and diagnostic tools, fostering innovation in the field of public health.

The CPHC is not just a physical link but a **pathway** towards health diplomacy, demonstrating the potential for collaboration in addressing global health challenges. It also stands as a testament to the power of visionary thinking and international collaboration in addressing crucial issues such as healthcare. This initiative not only enhances the healthcare landscape in Pakistan but also strengthens the bonds of friendship and cooperation between China and Pakistan. As the corridor continues to

evolve, its impact on the health sector and beyond is poised to be a **beacon** of success in Sino-Pak relations.

(787 words)

 New Words

corridor	/ˈkɒrɪˌdɔː/	n.	走廊；走廊地带
testament	/ˈtestəmənt/	n.	证明
eyewitness	/ˈaɪˌwɪtnɪs/	n.	目击者
conceive	/kənˈsiːv/	v.	认为；构想出
healthcare	/ˈhelθkeə(r)/	n.	医疗保健
multidisciplinary	/ˌmʌltɪˈdɪsɪˌplɪnərɪ/	adj.	多学科的
bolster	/ˈbəʊlstə/	v.	增强；巩固
array	/əˈreɪ/	n.	大量；陈列
auxiliary	/ɔːgˈzɪljərɪ/	adj.	辅助的；备用的
pharmaceutical	/ˌfɑːməˈsjuːtɪkəl/	adj.	制药的
underserved	/ˌʌndəˈsɜːvd/	adj.	服务水平低下的
accessibility	/əkˌsesəˈbɪləti/	n.	易使用性；可及性
leverage	/ˈliːvərɪdʒ/	n.	影响力；杠杆作用
		v.	举债经营；利用
diagnostic	/ˌdaɪəgˈnɒstɪk/	adj.	诊断的
streamline	/ˈstriːmˌlaɪn/	n.	流线
		v.	提高……效率
well-being	/ˈwel biːɪŋ/	n.	健康快乐
invaluable	/ɪnˈvæljuəbəl/	adj.	非常宝贵的
swift	/swɪft/	adj.	迅速的
hallmark	/ˈhɔːlˌmɑːk/	n.	标志；特征
showcase	/ˈʃəʊˌkeɪs/	v.	展示
		n.	玻璃陈列柜
withstand	/wɪðˈstænd/	v.	抵御
reciprocate	/prægˈmætɪk/	v.	报答；回报
stringent	/ˈstrɪndʒənt/	adj.	严格的
pandemic	/pandemic/	n.	流行病

epidemic	/ˈtaʊɪzəm/	n.	流行病；盛行，蔓延
accelerate	/əkˈseləreɪt/	v.	加速
vaccine	/ˈvæksiːn/	n.	疫苗
pathway	/ˈpɑːθˌweɪ/	n.	路径；途径
evolve	/ɪˈvɒlv/	v.	进化；逐步发展
beacon	/ˈbiːkən/	n.	信号灯；指路人

 ## Phrases and Expressions

in the wake of	在……之后
bring about	引起；导致
be exemplified by	以……为例
align with	与……一致
be attributed to	归因于
pave the way for	为……做准备

Section 2   Reading Comprehension

1. Directions: *Read the passage as quickly as you can. Answer the questions.*

(1) In what year was the idea of establishing the China-Pakistan Health Corridor (CPHC) conceived?

(2) What are some key stakeholders mentioned in the CPHC, reflecting its comprehensive approach to healthcare?

(3) Which cutting-edge technologies are mentioned in the passage as part of the technology integration initiative within the CPHC?

(4) Which specific international initiative does the passage mention as a context for collaborative efforts facilitated by the CPHC?

(5) What initiative is extended by the CPHC?

2. Directions: *Read the passage again. Decide whether the following statements are true (T) or false (F).*

(1) The author witnessed the notable bravery and collaboration of the Chinese nation during the coronavirus outbreak.   (   )

(2) The CPHC involves a multidisciplinary collaboration aimed at bolstering healthcare

infrastructure, knowledge exchange, and mutual cooperation between China and Pakistan. ( )

(3) The CPHC's key initiative is to privatize healthcare services in both China and Pakistan. ( )

(4) The CPHC represents a one-way transfer of knowledge from China to Pakistan. ( )

(5) China's success in responding to the coronavirus was a result of both the collective efforts of its people and the government's commitment to prioritizing the health and well-being of citizens. ( )

(6) The CPHC's impact is limited to the health sector, and it does not contribute to strengthening overall diplomatic ties between China and Pakistan. ( )

(7) Through the CPHC, BRI countries have the opportunity to enhance their capacity for addressing health challenges by leveraging Chinese expertise, sharing knowledge, and collaborating on healthcare infrastructure development. ( )

(8) The CPHC is primarily a physical link and does not play a role in addressing global health challenges or fostering international collaboration. ( )

What Do You Think?

3. **Directions:** *Discuss the followings in small groups or pairs. Then report to the class.*

(1) The CPHC utilizes advanced technologies like artificial intelligence, virtual reality, and big data in healthcare. How do you envision technology playing a role in improving healthcare services in your own life? Can you think of specific examples where technology could enhance healthcare delivery in your community?

(2) The passage mentions the establishment of mobile hospitals to extend medical services to remote areas. In your opinion, how might mobile healthcare initiatives address challenges in reaching underserved communities in your region? Can you think of other innovative ways to make healthcare more accessible?

(3) The CPHC involves collaboration between various stakeholders, including research centers, IT firms, and pharmaceutical industries. In your understanding, why is it important for different sectors to work together in improving healthcare? Can you think of examples from your own experiences where interdisciplinary collaboration could lead to positive outcomes in health?

(4) How can educational institutions contribute to promoting health awareness among students and their communities? Can you think of ways in which schools can actively

engage students in initiatives that foster a culture of health and well-being?

(5) The passage discusses collaboration leading to innovation in public health. As future educators, how might you collaborate with other educators to bring innovative approaches to health education in schools? Can you imagine joint projects or initiatives that could make a positive impact on students' health understanding and practices?

(6) The passage highlights collaboration in health diplomacy. How do you think educators can integrate global health concepts into the curriculum to broaden students' perspectives on healthcare? Can you envision ways to make global health relevant and engaging for students?

Vocabulary

4. Directions: *Read the following sentences. Search the passage for words that mean (near) the same as those underlined.*

(1) The school's wellness program aims to enhance the overall **health and happiness** of students by promoting healthy habits and positive social interactions.

(2) Her dedication to charity work stands as **evidence** to her commitment to making a positive impact on the community.

(3) His humility and generosity were the **most typical qualities** of his character, leaving a lasting impression on everyone he encountered.

(4) The city invested in creating more wheelchair ramps and tactile paving to improve **the ease of use** for all residents, ensuring a more inclusive urban environment.

(5) The lighthouse stood tall, acting as a **guiding signal** for ships, ensuring their safe navigation through the perilous waters.

5. Directions: *Complete the following sentences with the correct form of words from the passage.*

(1) The nonprofit organization focused its efforts on providing essential resources to **u** _____ communities, addressing gaps in access to education and healthcare.

(2) The **d** _____ software quickly analyzed the computer's performance, pinpointing the issues that needed attention to improve its speed and efficiency.

(3) In healthy relationships, partners **r** _____ each other's gestures of love and support, creating a harmonious and balanced bond.

(4) Technology continues to **e** _____ rapidly, with new innovations and advancements reshaping the way we live and work.

(5) The government implemented policies to **b** _____ the economy, providing financial support to struggling industries during challenging times.

(6) In response to the urgent situation, the emergency response team took **s** _____ action, deploying resources to the affected area within minutes.

(7) The architect worked tirelessly to **c** _____ a groundbreaking design that would blend innovation with functionality in the new building project.

(8) When faced with adversity, individuals with a strong mindset can **w** _____ challenges and emerge even more resilient.

6. Directions: *Complete the following sentences by selecting suitable phrases in the box.*

in the wake of	bring about	be exemplified by	align with
be attributed to	pave the way for		

(1) The company's new policies were designed to _____ industry standards, ensuring compliance and fostering positive relationships with stakeholders.

(2) The breakthrough in medical research can _____ years of dedicated study and the persistent pursuit of knowledge by the research team.

(3) The introduction of clean energy initiatives can _____ a reduction in carbon emissions and contribute to a more sustainable and environmentally friendly future.

(4) _____ the natural disaster, relief organizations mobilized quickly to provide aid and support to the affected communities.

PART **III** Understanding Global Issues

Strategies for Better Speaking

Speaking Skill: Coherence

When talking about a certain issue, a responsible speaker usually maintains a clear mind map on how he/she is to declare the focus and develop the idea with supporting details to achieve unity. Focus is the main idea of the topic or the most important information that the speaker wants to convey to the audience, while the supporting details are to illustrate the focus from different perspectives with examples, data, or arguments as further explanation or evidence. Besides the mind map, the speaker has to carefully arrange the logical order of the content in supporting details and use appropriate transitional expressions to help with unity and coherence of ideas presented.

Exercise

Directions: *Work with your partner and come up with a 3-minute story that features the topic of health, following the seven steps below. Please also refer to the four questions below as your prompts.*

Step 1: Browse the following questions and choose one that is interesting to you.

Step 2: Work with your partner and nail down a certain topic for the question(s) chosen.

Step 3: Discuss and write down the focus of your idea.

Step 4: Brainstorm the relevant details and major examples as further explanations, and search for data evidence when necessary.

Step 5: Select the details that well support your focus and draw a mind map.

Step 6: Arrange the details in a certain logical order to develop your ideas or arguments.

Step 7: Use appropriate transitions to clue your sentences before sharing it with the class.

(1) How has the COVID-19 pandemic influenced healthcare practices and policies, and what lessons have we learned from it?

(2) What is the most significant health issue or challenge you believe our society is currently facing, and how can it be addressed?

(3) How has the digital age, including social media and technology, affected people's mental well-being, and what can be done to mitigate potential negative impacts?

(4) Can you discuss the importance of setting and pursuing meaningful life goals for one's well-being?

Unit 8

Global Citizenship

PART ⅠⅠ Listening and Speaking

Section 1 Pre-listening Activity

Directions: Browse the questions below and discuss one of the following questions with your partner. List the key information, and share your opinion with the class.

(1) If you could visit any country in the world to learn about its culture and traditions, where would you go and why?

(2) Have you ever celebrated a holiday or festival from a culture different from your own? How was the experience?

(3) Can you think of a famous person from another country that you admire? What do you like about his/her?

(4) How does globalization impact the concept and practice of global citizenship?

(5) How does cross-cultural communication contribute to the development of global citizenship?

(6) How can technology facilitate global communication and collaboration among global citizens?

Section 2 Listening Comprehension

Passage One

Directions: Listen to the following passage. Choose the best answer to each question.

(1) What defines a global citizen according to the passage?

    A. Someone who isolates themselves from the world.

    B. Someone who is disconnected from global communities.

    C. Someone who is part of an emerging sustainable world community.

    D. Someone who prioritizes individual values over community values.

(2) Why do many people today identify themselves with being global citizens, as mentioned in the passage?

    A. Because they prefer local communities.

B. Because they want to disconnect from the world.

C. Because aspects of their lives are becoming globally connected.

D. Because they seek isolation from global influences.

(3) According to the passage, do global citizens need to give up their other citizenship identities?

A. Yes, it is a requirement.

B. No, it is not necessary.

C. Only if they travel extensively.

D. Only for certain responsibilities.

(4) What distinguishes global citizenship from national citizenship?

A. The need for special rights and privileges.

B. The need to travel to different countries.

C. A special passport and official title.

D. A connection to a broader global community.

(5) How does global citizenship influence change at regional, national and local levels, according to the passage?

A. By traveling to other countries.

B. By holding a special passport.

C. By positively contributing to the global community.

D. By learning different languages.

Passage Two

Directions: *Listen to the following passage. Choose the best answer to each question.*

(1) What is the primary focus of global citizenship, as mentioned in the passage?

A. Strong connection to one's community or nation.

B. Economic prosperity and growth.

C. Civic actions that promote a better world and future.

D. Discrimination and exclusivity.

(2) How is sustainable development defined in the passage?

A. Development at the expense of the environment.

B. Meeting the present needs without compromising future generations.

C. Focusing solely on economic issues.

D. Ignoring the interconnectedness between peoples.

(3) According to the passage, what does sustainable development emphasize in terms of the relationship between development and the environment?

A. Development at the expense of the environment.

B. Ignoring the environmental aspects of development.

C. Focusing solely on economic and social issues.

D. Balancing the demands of the environment, economy, and society.

(4) According to the passage, what are some of the global challenges that global citizenship and sustainable development aim to address?

A. Nationalism and regional conflicts.

B. Economic inequality and discrimination.

C. Environmental degradation, terrorism, and conflicts.

D. Exclusivity and radicalization.

(5) What is the goal of global citizenship and sustainable development, as mentioned in the passage?

A. Promoting economic growth at any cost.

B. Triggering fundamental changes for peaceful and sustainable societies.

C. Ignoring global challenges and conflicts.

D. Exclusively focusing on national interests.

 ## Strategies for Better Listening

Listening Skill: Taking Effective Notes

While listening to a passage, the listener needs to understand and memorize important information within a very short time span because new information keeps flowing. Therefore, taking effective notes may help a lot when answering comprehension questions.

To show a clear structure as well as relationship between main ideas and specific details, it is better to indent the notes, meaning "move your text to the right". To save time while taking notes, write the key words instead of complete sentences; More often, abbreviations and symbols work more efficiently provided you are familiar with the abbreviated forms and symbols. A listener is encouraged to create your own list of symbols.

Exercise

Directions: *Browse the following examples. Write the symbols for the words and phrases taken from the listening passages in Section 2.*

=: like, equals, means (in defining a term)

#: unlike, not the same as

#: number

+: plus, in addition, and

↑: increase

↓: decrease

→: causes (as in A → B)

∴: therefore, as a result

w/: with

w/o: without

re: concerning or regarding

...

(1) Being a global citizen *does not mean* that you have to give up the other citizenship identities you already have, e.g. your country citizenship, your identities in your local community, and religious, or ethnic group.

_____ *does not mean*

(2) *Unlike citizenship*, which involves special rights, privileges and responsibilities related to "belonging" to a particular nation or state, the global citizenship concept is based on the idea we are connected not just with one country but with a broader global community.

_____ *unlike citizenship*

(3) What is sustainable development? Sustainable development *can be understood as* "development that meets the needs of the present without comprising the ability of future generations to meet their own needs".

_____ *can be understood as*

PART II Reading

Section 1 Pre-reading Activity

1. Directions: *The passage you are going to read talks about "biculturalism". In groups, discuss the following questions.*

(1) What does "biculturalism" mean to you? Can you think of any personal experiences or examples from your community that reflect a blend of two cultures?

(2) In what ways do you believe biculturalism can enrich a society? Are there potential challenges or misunderstandings that might arise from embracing multiple cultural influences?

(3) Reflect on your own cultural background. How do you balance the traditions and values of your culture with those of the broader society you live in? Can you identify any instances where cultural clashes or harmonies have shaped your identity?

2. Directions: *The following are a few lines from the passage. In your opinion, what are they talking about?*

(1) "Students at Kensington Wade school in England speak English for half of their school days and Chinese for the other half..."

(2) "To immerse someone in Chinese learning is to apply the language to instruction in a variety of subjects..."

(3) "An early immersion enables students to develop greater language comprehension and production abilities with a very natural accent..."

(4) "... students are taught to appreciate the beauty behind the differences..."

Chinese Immersion Program Promotes Biculturalism①

Students at Kensington Wade school in England speak English for half of their school days and Chinese for the other half; whether they are doing a language lesson or not. On Chinese-speaking days, classes, including mathematics, science, art and humanities, are taught in Chinese by native Chinese-speaking teachers. The "Half English, Half Chinese" **formula** makes Kensington Wade the first and only **bilingual** English-Chinese **prep school** in Europe.

Located in the Hammersmith district of West London, the school has attracted more than 100 students, aged between three and eleven. They come from Chinese, British, French, Russian, German and Indian backgrounds. The school has grown from **humble** origins. When it first opened in 2017, there were just 15 children on its books.

"The decision to start the first-ever English-Chinese bilingual prep school, not just in the UK but in Europe, was taken because we felt there was a huge need to give children of this country the ability to speak, live, and work in a world where China was a hugely, hugely important presence," said Jo Wallace, the school's principal and founding **head teacher**.

While Chinese is taught widely in the UK, mostly in secondary schools through the Mandarin Excellence Program, what makes Kensington Wade unique is its foreign language teaching method, **immersion** education, which is a "new, **pioneering**, and progressing" model, the school's **Deputy** Head and Head of Chinese Program Wang Jing said.

To immerse someone in Chinese learning is to apply the language to instruction in a variety of subjects, which **converts** Chinese into a "**by-product** of content teaching", said Wang.

"Sometimes, a child is not really interested in learning how I would use Chinese characters to make a sentence, but they really want to figure out how this science project would go, or what the results are going to be. And if that lesson is **delivered** in Chinese, they will be learning the language without realizing, oh, I am actually learning a language."

An early immersion enables students to develop greater language comprehension and production abilities with a very natural accent, which count as a **linguistically** competent advantage, said Wang, while at the same time, **biculturalism** is embraced by the children at **tender** ages, as teachers use China as a context to teach history,

---

① From *China Daily*.

geography, art, and so on.

In humanities classrooms, to illustrate the gender **stereotyping** ascribed to females and to talk about how some of them have broken the **bias**, Wang's English-teaching partner cites the world-renowned Florence Nightingale, the founder of modern nursing, and Wang talks about Hua Mulan, the Chinese folk **heroine** who took her aged father's place in the **conscription** for the army by **disguising** herself as a man.

In the geography unit, the Yangtze River, China's longest river, is compared with the Nile in Africa, which explains how rivers can be seen as the **cradles** of human civilization. "Children are always comparing. So, they do know the world is not a **one-man** story, they do know there are people who do things differently, and they will use that kind of skill to come to their own decisions. They have greater critical thinking skills to help them make good decisions," Wang said.

And students are taught to appreciate the beauty behind the differences, by learning the two languages that represent the East and the West, said Xiang Yang, assistant head of Chinese and **coordinator** of the art, design and technology department.

"For example, dragons in our Chinese culture **signify auspiciousness**, but in the West, they are perceived as **vicious** and scary monsters. Our children are exposed to totally different cultural backgrounds, and they **sweep** those changes very quickly on a daily basis. In the end, they show more **empathy** toward different situations," Xiang said.

For Xiang, being exposed to differences at an age when students are far from realizing how the world runs, is a **privilege**, because accepting diversity is needed to foster global citizenship.

Wallace said she wants her school to keep sending out the message that empathy and understanding should be **nurtured**, and for people to increasingly realize that having a school like Kensington Wade, which nurtures students with bilingual and bicultural brains, is vital.

"Hopefully, one day, we won't be the only one," she said.

(705 words)

 New Words

formula	/ˈfɔːmjʊlə/	*n.*	方案；公式
bilingual	/ baɪˈlɪŋgwəl /	*adj.*	双语的

humble	/ˈhʌmbəl/	adj.	谦卑的；谦逊的
immersion	/ɪˈmɜːʃən/	n.	沉浸；浸泡
pioneering	/ˌpaɪəˈnɪərɪŋ/	adj.	开创性的
deputy	/ˈdepjʊtɪ/	adj.	副的
convert	/kənˈvɜːt /	v.	转变
by-product	/ˈbaɪprɒdʌkt/	n.	副产品
deliver	/dɪˈlɪvə/	v.	发表；实现；递送
linguistically	/lɪŋˈgwɪstɪkli/	adv.	语言上的；语言学方面
biculturalism	/baɪˈkʌltʃərəlɪzəm/	n.	二元文化
tender	/ˈtendə/	adj.	温柔的；幼小的
stereotype	/ˈsteriətaɪp/	n.	刻板印象
bias	/ˈbaɪəs/	n.	偏见
heroine	/ˈherəʊɪn/	n.	女主人公；女英雄
conscription	/kənˈskrɪpʃən/	n.	征用；征兵入伍
disguise	/dɪsˈgaɪz/	v.	伪装；装扮
cradle	/ˈkreɪdəl/	n.	摇篮
one-man	/ˌwʌn ˈmæn/	adj.	一人控制的
coordinator	/kəʊˈɔːdɪneɪtə(r)/	n.	协调人；统筹者
signify	/ˈsɪgnɪˌfaɪ/	v.	表示；意味着
auspiciousness	/ɔːˈspɪʃəsnɪs/	n.	吉兆；幸运
vicious	/ˈvɪʃəs/	adj.	凶残的；恶毒的
sweep	/swiːp/	v.	打扫；传播
empathy	/ˈempəθɪ/	n.	共情
privilege	/ˈprɪvəlɪdʒ/	n.	特权；荣幸
nurture	/ˈnɜːtʃə/	v.	培养；培育
hopefully	/ˈhəʊpfʊlɪ/	adv.	但愿

 Phrases and Expressions

prep school		私立预备学校
head teacher		校长
figure out		想出；弄明白
ascribe... to		把……归于

come to a decision	作出决定
perceive as	将……视为
expose... to	暴露于
on a daily basis	每天

Section 2　Reading Comprehension

1. Directions: *Read the passage as quickly as you can. Answer the questions.*

(1) What age range do the students at Kensington Wade fall into?

(2) How many students were there when Kensington Wade school first opened in 2017?

(3) Who is the principal and founding head teacher of Kensington Wade?

(4) Who is the Chinese folk heroine discussed in the passage, known for taking her aged father's place in the conscription for the army?

(5) Who is mentioned as the founder of modern nursing in the context of breaking gender stereotypes in the humanities classroom?

2. Directions: *Read the passage again. Decide whether the following statements true (T) or false (F).*

(1) Kensington Wade is the only bilingual English-Chinese prep school in Europe. (　　)

(2) The school was established to prepare children for a world where China's global importance is significant.　(　　)

(3) Jo Wallace, the school's principal, emphasizes the importance of teaching Mandarin through the Mandarin Excellence Program.　(　　)

(4) The passage suggests that teaching Chinese through practical applications, like science projects, aligns with an immersive language education model.　(　　)

(5) The geography unit in the school compares the Yangtze River with the Amazon River in South America.　(　　)

(6) In Western culture, dragons are seen as creatures associated with good fortune.

(　　)

(7) Exposure to diverse cultural backgrounds at an early age can lead children to develop empathy towards various situations.　(　　)

(8) The primary message Wallace wants her school to convey is the importance of

nurturing empathy and understanding among students.　　　　　　(　)

What Do You Think?

3. Directions: *Discuss the followings in small groups or pairs. Then report to the class.*

(1) How do you think the bilingual education model, where students switch between English and Chinese instruction, can benefit students in their daily lives?

(2) In what ways might the immersion education method, as described in the text, enhance students' language learning experience compared with traditional language teaching approaches?

(3) Considering the diverse backgrounds of students at Kensington Wade, how might the exposure to both Eastern and Western cultures contribute to the development of biculturalism among the students?

(4) Reflecting on the humanities classrooms discussed in the passage, how might incorporating stories of historical figures from both Eastern and Western cultures help challenge gender stereotypes and promote a more inclusive perspective?

(5) The passage emphasizes the students' ability to compare and appreciate differences in the world. How do you think this skill of comparing and contrasting cultures can be applied in students' daily interactions and decision-making?

(6) Discuss the statement that "accepting diversity is needed to foster global citizenship". How can educational institutions play a role in promoting a sense of global citizenship among students, and why is it important in today's interconnected world?

Vocabulary

4. Directions: *Read the following sentences. Search the passage for words that mean the same as those underlined.*

(1) It's important to recognize that making assumptions based on **fixed and oversimplified notions** can lead to unfair judgments and perpetuate biases.

(2) Virtual reality technology offers a unique **deep involvement** experience, transporting users to different environments with a heightened sense of presence.

(3) In the counseling session, the therapist demonstrated **a deep understanding** of the client's emotions and feelings, creating a safe space for healing.

(4) The team's collaborative approach fostered a culture of knowledge exchange, with increased productivity emerging as a positive **incidental result** of their mutual support.

(5) Growing up in a diverse neighborhood, Maria developed a strong sense of **dual cultural identity**, seamlessly integrating elements from both her native and adopted cultures.

5. Directions: *Complete the following sentences with the correct form of words from the passage.*

(1) The scientist worked tirelessly to **c** _____ the experimental data into meaningful conclusions that could contribute to advancements in the field.

(2) Yesterday's announcement by the CEO **s** _____ a major shift in the company's strategic direction.

(3) Cultivating a garden requires ongoing attention and care to **n** _____ healthy plants.

(4) Last Halloween, she **d** _____ herself as a mysterious witch and delighted in the reactions of trick-or-treaters.

(5) In the face of success, it is essential to stay **h** _____ and continue learning and growing.

(6) The couple is excited to start their new life together, and the sunny weather on their wedding day is considered an **a** _____ sign.

(7) It is a **p** _____ to work with such a talented and dedicated team, and I appreciate the opportunities for growth and collaboration.

(8) The journalist strives to present news without **b** _____, ensuring a fair and balanced perspective on current events.

6. Directions: *Complete the following sentences by selecting suitable phrases in the box.*

figure out	ascribe... to	come to a decision	perceive as
expose... to	on a daily basis		

(1) Our team meets _____ to discuss ongoing projects and address any emerging issues.

(2) After hours of discussion, the committee has finally _____ regarding the new company policy.

(3) I _____ the solution to the complex mathematical problem I've been working on for weeks.

(4) The success of the company can _____ the innovative leadership and strategic decision-making of its CEO.

PART III Understanding Global Issues

Strategies for Better Speaking

Speaking Skill: Conducting Interviews on Campus

A university is like an anthill, crowed with students from different cultures and backgrounds. To promote understanding among students, teachers may encourage their students to conduct a series of surveys or interviews. For preparation, the interviewer needs to clarify the purpose of the interview and design questions carefully to allow enough space for the interviewees. More importantly, learn about the interviewees regarding their customs and taboos to avoid awkwardness during interviews. Lastly, practicing active listening while the interviewees are speaking is highly recommended so that potential valuable ideas can be revealed.

Exercise

Directions: *Work with your partner and conduct an interview that features the topic of global citizenship on campus, following the seven steps below. Please also refer to the four questions below as your prompts.*

Step 1: Browse the following four questions and choose two that are interesting to you.

Step 2: Work with your partner to decide on the focus of your interview.

Step 3: Brainstorm the best candidate for your interview.

Step 4: Learn about the interviewee and design the interview questions carefully.

Step 5: Seek help from your teacher if you are to interview overseas students.

Step 6: Make an appointment with your interviewee and conduct the interview.

Step 7: Wrap up the responses and prepare a video report of your findings.

(1) What does the term "global citizenship" mean to you, and how do you think it has evolved over time?

(2) How can individuals contribute to global citizenship in their everyday lives, regardless of their cultural background?

(3) How can travel and exposure to different cultures contribute to the development of a global mindset?

(4) Can you identify any global issues or challenges that you believe require immediate attention and collective action from global citizens? Please provide specific examples.